What They Never Taught Me in Principal's School

The Value of Experience Cannot Be Overestimated

Michael Connolly

ROWMAN & LITTLEFIELD EDUCATION
Lanham • Boulder • New York • Toronto • Plymouth, UK

Published in the United States of America
by Rowman & Littlefield Education
A Division of Rowman & Littlefield Publishers, Inc.
A wholly owned subsidary of The Rowman & Littlefield Publishing Group, Inc.
4501 Forbes Boulevard, Suite 200, Lanham, Maryland 20706
www.rowmaneducation.com

Estover Road
Plymouth PL6 7PY
United Kingdom

British Library Cataloguing in Publication Information Available

Library of Congress Cataloging-in-Publication Data

Connolly, Michael, 1942-
    What they never taught me in principal's school : the value of experience cannot
be overestimated / Michael Connolly.
        p. cm.
    Includes bibliographical references.
    ISBN 978-1-60709-307-7 (cloth : alk. paper) -- ISBN 978-1-60709-308-4 (pbk. : alk.
    paper) -- ISBN 978-1-60709-309-1 (electronic)
  1. School principals--United States. 2. Educational leadership--United States. I.
Title.
    LB2831.92.C66 2009
    371.2'012--dc22   2009027160

To my wife Brie who has always supported me through the many challenges of being a principal and of writing this book.

Contents

Acknowledgements

How can someone entering a new leadership position survive long enough to learn how to deal with the responsibility of such a position, particularly at times when, like Atlas, he may feel like he is carrying the weight of the world on his shoulders? The support and advice of a good mentor is invaluable in those situations.

I have been fortunate to have had four stellar mentors in my career: Howie Gilmore, who was principal when I accepted my first school leadership position as an assistant principal at Groton-Dunstable Regional Secondary School; Ed Martin, superintendent of the Mascenic Regional School District where I first served as a principal; Dick Crystal, who became superintendent while I served as Middle School principal in Swampscott, Massachusetts; and Paul DeMinico, who was head of the International School of Bangkok where I had my first international school leadership experience.

I give my heartfelt thanks to each of them for showing me where many of the leadership minefields were located and for putting me back together again when I, on more than one occasion, walked into one despite their counsel and blew myself up.

Over the years I have also been fortunate in having several people encourage me to continue on with my second professional passion—writing. I owe a special thanks to my wife Brie for her loving support and encouragement in this area. I want to thank David Bucknell who published many of my articles on education in his online journal *The International Education Daily* and Barrie Jo Price who encouraged me to send articles to NAESP's Principal's Electronic Newsdesk. I am deeply grateful to Lee Greene, former editor of *Principal* magazine, for publishing and encouraging my work and to Debra Brydon for her assistance in having my work published in Australia.

A special thanks to Kevin Haverty and Burt Goodrich for agreeing to read the original manuscript of this book and for offering me so many excellent suggestions for making it better.

Although I have titled my book *What They Never Taught Me in Principal's School*, in part because it's a beguiling title but also to acknowledge that no amount of schooling can ever fully prepare anyone for the challenges he will face as a school leader, I have been fortunate in my career to attend a number of excellent principal's schools. I am deeply grateful to the faculty and staff of Antioch New England College in Keene, New Hampshire, where I received my certification as a school administrator. I also owe a sincere debt of gratitude to the members of The Principal's Center at Harvard University and to the New Hampshire Principals' Association; I attended leadership institutes conducted by both of these organizations and learned a great many useful lessons at these principal's schools.

And finally, I cannot adequately express my appreciation to Tom Koerner of Rowman & Littlefield Education whose patience, encouragement, and support have made this publication possible. A simple thank you, insufficient as it may be, will have to do. Thank you, Tom.

Preface

When I was drafted in 1968 and sent to Vietnam, one of the first things the veterans there did was to take all new recruits to a section of base camp where they had replicated a minefield in which all the different explosive devices used in the Vietnam War were concealed. They walked us through the field and showed us all the ways we could blow ourselves and others up if we weren't observant and careful. It was a valuable experience. It was a life-saving experience.

There are minefields that principals and other educational leaders have to walk through almost every day. Those who've walked through them and survived owe it to those who will follow to share their survival strategies with them.

Research studies and educational theories of leadership practices taught in graduate schools and workshops are helpful and should not be dismissed, but what emerging leaders need are the stories and advice of mature leaders whose knowledge and experience have been forged in the daily challenges of leadership. That is why I titled this book *What They Never Taught Me in Principal's School*; it talks about lessons a principal can't learn in textbooks or master in university classrooms or professional development workshops. The learning must come through living the experiences. And while the actual experiences I describe cannot be duplicated for the reader in the pages of this or any book, the lessons learned, both good and bad, can be passed on.

In this book I share with you many of my own experiences, survival strategies, and stories of the minefields that I walked into, around, and through during my career as a school leader. And while I wrote this book from a principal's perspective for principals and aspiring principals, the topics covered and the skills discussed are broad enough so that they can be helpful to other school leaders including private school heads, superintendents, curriculum and technology coordinators, department heads, school board members, and even, I might be so bold to suggest, business and political leaders who have an interest in education and in teaching others in their own professions.

Ralph Nader once said that the true measure of a leader is not how many followers he begat, but how many leaders he begat. That is as true for those of us who are retiring from the ranks of active school leadership as it is for those of you who remain in it. It is my hope that in writing this book I can help you become a more effective leader by making you more aware of the challenges you will face along the path to your leadership success and by giving you the confidence that you have, or can get, the tools you'll need to meet them. Do not fear challenges or allow yourself to be overwhelmed by obstacles. Remember that there would be little need for leaders if the path to success was always safe and easy. On the other hand, don't underestimate the difficulty of the challenges you face as an educational leader.

I have another hope in writing this book and sharing my stories. Those of us in leadership positions know how lonely and burdensome the life of a leader can become. But too often we are our own worst enemies when it comes to this; we make the loneliness and the burden greater by keeping the stories of our challenges, our hopes, our disappointments, and even our successes to ourselves. Over the course of our careers we become accomplished stoics.

In writing this book and sharing my stories, I hope to encourage other leaders to share the stories of the challenges they've had to confront, the hopes they hold, the disappointments they've faced, and the victories they've won. That is one of the ways, I believe, that leaders beget and sustain other leaders. It is also a good way to sustain oneself.

THE ORGANIZATION OF THE BOOK

Most of the chapters in this book deal with leadership matters that a principal will deal with within the walls of his school. Beginning with chapter 17, however, I talk about issues that principals should consider as they face their broader responsibility for providing leadership in their communities, the nation, and the world.

In chapter 22, I take the liberty of introducing some random thoughts and observations that I believe are worthwhile for leaders to consider. As I've discovered in writing this book, anyone who tries to chronicle all the things they didn't learn in principal's school will end up composing a library rather than a book.

A brief summary of each chapter is given here; I encourage you to skip around and read and re-read chapters as the need arises.

Finally, you will notice that none of the chapters in this book are particularly long. That is intentional. Having been a school leader myself for over twenty years, I have a great respect for the demands on leaders' time. With that in mind, I have adopted a writer's version of Franklin Delano Roosevelt's advice on how to give a good speech: "Be sincere, be brief, and be seated." I've tried to be sincere, be informative, and be brief. I hope I've succeeded.

CHAPTER SUMMARIES

The Principal's Toolbox—Using an anecdote taken from Stephen King's book *On Writing* this chapter describes the kinds of tools principals need to keep in the top drawer of their leadership toolbox where they will be handy and ready for use. Tools included are listening, reflection, and planning tools.

Are You Listening or Only Hearing?—Lyndon Johnson said it well. "You ain't learnin' nothin' when you're talkin'." But there is more to listening than merely hearing what someone's saying. This chapter gives several suggestions for building good listening skills.

Time Out for Reflection—This chapter reminds principals that reflection is not something that a leader does when he has time for it; it is something he makes time for.

Principals Need to Stay Focused—Focus should be like a bench vice that keeps a principal's and the school faculty's work from slipping off into areas that do little to further the school's mission and core values.

Aylmer's Mistake and the Process of School Change—Using the example of Aylmer's mistake in Nathaniel Hawthorne's "The Birthmark," this chapter argues that along with change principals have to ensure continuity, order, and regularity in their school environments or everyone in the school will suffer.

It's Time to Discipline School Reform—Reform efforts in many schools look and feel like an afternoon on amusement park bumper cars with one school initiative careening into another. This chapter uses several anecdotes, including the lesson of the Mason jar, to argue that effective change efforts are evolutionary rather than revolutionary and gives advice on how to discipline the reform process in a school.

Harried Principals Aren't Helpful Principals—This chapter explains why principals have to develop patience and perseverance in order to get better results and gives them some strategies for doing it.

So You're the Principal; Well, What Have You Done for Yourself Today?—Using the story of a custodian I found sleeping in a storeroom during his lunch break, this chapter points out why principals need to learn to look after themselves, not just others, and gives five suggestions for how to do it.

They Never Told Me That in Principal's School!—This chapter deals with some of the myths of the principal's position: power versus responsibility, reaction versus overreaction, and the imprudence of the "my door is always open" philosophy.

A Reality Check for a New School Leader—An eye-opening personal experience serves as the background for my views on why faculty members have difficulty understanding the role of the school leader and how principals should handle this.

"Say Something Nice to Me": A Strategy for Dealing with the Chronically Cranky—One of the most energy-depleting challenges school leaders face is listening to the chronic complaining of individuals who seem never to be satisfied. Find a suggestion here for how to deal with this challenge and those individuals.

Principals Must Avoid Doggy Behavior—There is a particular behavior principals should avoid when they take a new leadership position. This chapter identifies that behavior and offers a few strategies for avoiding it.

The Courage of Educational Leaders—This chapter argues that educational leaders need to talk more openly about why courage is an essential component of educational leadership and describes the many instances in which principals may be called upon to use it.

A Principal Must Protect the Social Ecology of the School—This chapter maintains that schools are social habitats every bit as fragile as environmental habitats and that some of the initiatives that attempt to improve schools are in reality pushing more and more of them onto the endangered species list.

When Will We Ever Learn?—This chapter offers some suggestions, other than university courses and professional development workshops, for promoting your own and your faculty's learning and growth.

Discipline Isn't a Dirty Word—Ask a student how they define discipline and invariably you get the answer: punishment. And too often the students are right. In this chapter you'll find some suggestions for changing the perception of discipline from a negative to a positive.

"Seek the Story Within": Interview to Reveal the Heart of a Teacher—Interviews for open positions in your school should reveal more than just if a candidate is professionally qualified. Here are some interviewing strategies designed to reveal the candidate's inner depth.

What a Revolting Development This Is!: The Homework Rebellion—There is a great deal of discussion about the value of homework these days. This chapter offers some thoughts on why homework is valuable and provides some tools for parents to use to ensure it is valuable.

How Do You Spell Friendship? The Intergenerational Spelling Bee—Students and senior citizens may feel like they are opposite poles of the earth, but when we build a bridge between them, they discover they have more in common than they realized. The result is friendship and support of each other.

Educators' Responsibility for Creating a Public—Neil Postman said that education doesn't serve a public; it creates one. So what kind of public does the United States and the world need, and what is an educational leader's role in creating such a public?

Should Schools Offer Parent Training?—When schools reach out to parents in ways that go beyond parent conferences, that reach out can result in reduced frustration, anger, and isolation and promote better understanding between parents and teachers.

Musings—Brief reflections on issues related to school leadership.

We Are the Lucky Ones—Despite the challenges and frustrations of our leadership role, we have reason to be grateful for being able to do the work we do.

A PERSONAL NOTE TO MY READERS

Over my years in education, I have been privileged to work with many female as well as male school leaders whom I admire and respect. In writing this book, I struggled with which pronoun(s) I should use. In an early draft I used *s/he* in many sentences but heard that this merely served as an unpleasant distraction for readers. In another draft I alternated the use of *she* and *he* but found that such a technique often confused me and, I feared, would confuse my readers. So in the end I settled for the generic pronoun *he* since I am male. But any reader of this book should feel comfortable using *she* in virtually all instances where I have used *he*.

1

The Principal's Toolbox

On a flight from Bangkok, Thailand, to San Jose, Costa Rica, I began reading Stephen King's *On Writing*. I needed to get a grip on something more substantial than the latest Hollywood blockbuster in-flight movie. Changing jobs after eight years had that kind of effect on me. King's book proved to be funny, irreverent, and elegantly written. Nothing unusual there; this is, after all, Stephen King.

Part memoir and part handbook for practicing writers, *On Writing* is an engaging read even if you are not interested in becoming a writer, which I am, or particularly interested in Stephen King novels, which, I confess, I am not. In it, King serves up a banquet of tantalizing thoughts about what makes those who practice the craft of writing successful.

Now, as it happens, I'd been thinking about what it takes to practice my own craft well. I'm a school principal. So I found King's observations on his craft appealing. In particular I found one of King's metaphors particularly apt for the thoughts I was having about moving to a new job. The metaphor? A toolbox.

Let's face it, a school leader is either a builder or a maintenance man, often both, and in either role he needs to carry a good set of tools. A leader without an adequate set of tools is like a carpenter working without his toolbox. Over the past few months as I prepared to transition from one job to another I'd been mentally inventorying my personal stash of leadership tools trying to imagine which of them I might be called upon to use in my new position.

I do not mean to suggest in what follows that the tools I describe in this chapter are the only equipment a school leader needs. I'd need to write a set of encyclopedias to record all of those. I mean only to suggest that if these tools are not among the everyday equipment the leader carries with him to his job, he needs to acquire them. To build an educational vision, to repair a damaged one, or to construct the scaffolding necessary to support a school's mission, a leader must have *at least* these tools and must learn to use them well. So having said that let me lift the lid of the toolbox and reveal what should be there.

The *ability to listen* is as basic a tool for a school leader as a saw or a hammer is for a carpenter. Any leader who has not trained himself to listen, not just to hear, is in for trouble, and trouble will not be long in coming. Most of us fancy ourselves good listeners, but we may be deceiving ourselves. How many people listening to CNN broadcasts about the war with Iraq heard commentators talking about weapons of mass destruction and "smart" bombs and caught the implication that these smart bombs weren't to be considered in the same category as weapons of mass destruction? How many questioned the idea that bombs can be smart?

Our ability to listen is often compromised by two problematic assumptions that I'll have more to say about in the next chapter. The first assumption is that listening is a natural everyday exercise and is easy. Wrong. The second assumption is that as a listener we must always be prepared to respond to what we have heard. Wrong again! God gave us two ears and only one mouth for a reason. It should be obvious he intended that we should be listening twice as much and speaking half as often. Every school leader needs to recognize that listening is one of the most essential tools he can put into his toolbox. This is an everyday tool that a leader must keep sharpened and on the top level of the toolbox.

The next tool should be on the top level of a school principal's toolbox as well. It is the *reflection* tool. Every leader needs to cultivate the ability to reflect upon what he is doing, why he is doing it, and if it is what he should be doing. If a school leader does not set aside time for reflection and does not take steps to preserve that time, he will find himself responding only to the urgency of each moment with little control over where that urgency is leading him and the school.

I am not suggesting here that any school leader can ignore the urgent demands of the job. If he does that, he will find himself at the head of the unemployment line rather than at the helm of a school. On the other hand, if a leader responds *only* to the urgency of each moment, he will eventually lose touch with the educational aims of the school—or at least forfeit the time to address them. Everything is urgent to someone in the school community.

A leader must be able to distinguish between the urgent and the important, even if others cannot. "There must be a time," wrote Thomas Merton, "when a man who makes plans stops and asks himself do those plans have any meaning" (p. 260). This is the school leader's time for reflection, and he can ill afford to have this tool lost or stolen

Which brings us to the next tool: *focus*. That time for reflection I just spoke of is necessary to keep this tool within reach and serviceable. Without a clear focus a school may be an industrious place, but as Henry David Thoreau pointed out, ants are industrious. What is important is what we are industrious about. This is where focus comes in.

Focus is the bench vice that keeps the school and its people anchored in the grip of what they should be doing. Focus forces us to separate the superficial from the substantial even when we are pushed and pulled hither and yon by forces that would have us do other things, or worse, everything. Focus guarantees that the mission of the school won't be buried under an avalanche of other demands: budgets, school lunch programs, school board meetings, public relations campaigns, school building projects, and on and on.

Finally, there is one last tool that I must include before I close the lid on the toolbox for now: the *planning* tool. It does not matter here what we call the planning tool: strategic planning, action planning, or whatever other smarmy name we choose to give it. The point is that a school leader needs to know not only how to plan but also how to teach other school personnel to plan and to follow the plan.

Most leaders know at least the basics of how to plan and have templates for doing it. That is not the problem. The challenge lies not so much in acquiring this tool but in learning how to use it. Many school plans are so ambitious that they have no chance of success. Groaning with the weight of multiple initiatives and unrealistic timelines, they are prescriptions for failure and disappointment. Such plans seldom account for what is working in the school and for what existing foundations a new plan can be built upon. While they may identify the resources that will be needed to accomplish the goals, they seldom do an assessment of whether or not such resources will be available in the amount that will be required.

Take *time*, for instance. Time, like fossil fuels, is one of our most precious resources and one whose reserves we can easily deplete. Most school plans grossly underestimate the amount of time school personnel (teachers in particular) have to devote to them. In addition, the architects of many school plans fail to ask themselves if the people who must implement their plans are emotionally as well as intellectually ready to implement them, and if they are not, how much time and what resources will be needed to get them ready. When the planning tool is used like this, or more accurately, misused like this, the resulting plan may be visionary, especially if by visionary we mean unrealistic, but it will also be unachievable.

Learning to use the planning tool requires that one learn not just what to put into a plan, but what to keep out of it. Remember that celebrated but seldom practiced activity that we architects of change call "selective abandonment"? It is a very functional and fit planning instrument. We need to bring it back and use it. As a matter of fact let's put it into our toolbox and on the top shelf.

School principals seldom know from day to day which tools they will be called upon to use, so I recommend to you the advice Stephen King received from his Uncle Oren on the subject of being prepared for anything. When young Stevie asked his uncle why he lugged a big heavy toolbox out of the garage to repair a screen when all he needed was a screwdriver, Uncle Oren replied:

"Yeah, but Stevie, . . . I didn't know what else I might find to do once I got out here, did I? It's best to have your tools with you. If you don't, you're apt to find something you didn't expect and get discouraged" (p. 114).

That's good advice for school leaders as well as carpenters.

2

Are You Listening or Only Hearing?

I'm driving along New Hampshire Route 9 with a sense of anticipation. I'm on my way to do the grocery shopping. I should be rehearsing my list of things to buy; I sometimes return from these excursions only to realize I've forgotten something important. Instead, I'm looking for the three wild turkeys I saw dining along this stretch of road yesterday. If they are still here a month from now it's likely someone will be dining on them. This is hunter's territory. Suddenly I'm distracted by something else.

On a stark white bulletin board with plain black lettering that sits outside a local mom-and-pop store advertising today's specials, I'm confronted with this intriguing question: "Are you listening or only hearing?" OK, so it doesn't have the folksy pizzazz of Lyndon Johnson's "You ain't learnin' nothin' when you're talkin'." Nonetheless it's arresting. It reminds me that one of the best tools we humans have is our ability to listen. But how many of us use that tool effectively? The sign along Route 9 seems to confirm my suspicion. Not many.

We humans operate on faulty assumptions about listening; assumptions not shared by our brothers and sisters in the animal kingdom. Those assumptions impair our ability to listen well and often get us into trouble. My guess is that those turkeys will hear the sounds of fall approaching and listen for the noise of hunters cleaning their rifles and be long gone by the time hunting season opens. But what about us; can we humans learn to listen carefully enough to stay out of trouble?

In the previous chapter I mentioned the two problematic assumptions that interfere with listening. The first is that listening is natural and thus easy. But while hearing is natural and easy, listening is not; it is an acquired skill. Listening demands willing attention to what is being said and how it's being said and even, at times, to what is *not* said. Such attention is not necessarily required of hearing. We hear many things that we don't pay much attention to: background noise, radio blabber, and the sound of humming machinery to name a few. But when we listen to someone, we choose to pay attention to someone's words, tone of voice, and even to the emotions that may lie beneath.

The second assumption is that when we listen we need to give a response to what we've heard. The fallacy of this assumption was demonstrated to me dramatically in my own home.

I arrived home one day to find one of my sons fulminating about a bill the dentist's office had sent him for a missed appointment. This particular son is a redhead and anyone who is old enough to have seen a Maureen O'Hara movie understands that the fulminations of redheads can be impressive. I listened for a while, or rather thought I was listening, as my son railed on about the injustice of it all. Finally, calling up my most diplomatic counseling skills, I began explaining to him that he was in this case paying for the dentist's time not his service since he had failed to cancel the appointment and chose to be a "no show." I was well into my dissertation on the economics of a service provider's time when my son interrupted me.

"Dad I don't need your advice on this. I know I was wrong. I know what I did was stupid. I just need to get out my frustration."

Until then I had been hearing what my son had been saying but not listening to him.

When we listen to people, truly listen to them, we need not feel compelled to give them advice. Listening alone gives them two of the greatest gifts one person can offer another: the gift of our time and our attention. People who are listened to know they are respected even when they understand we don't agree with them or when the problem they brought remains unsolved. Our advice, if we have advice to give, may be valuable or not, but our willingness to listen is priceless.

Nature has endowed most of us with excellent faculties for hearing, yet we remain "hard of listening." Fortunately this disability is not irreversible. With commitment and practice we can join the ranks of those who listen as well as hear.

SUGGESTIONS

- Position yourself so that it is obvious that you are giving the speaker your undivided attention. Face the speaker and let him see that you are attending to what he's saying.

- Listen not just to the words but to the emotion behind them as well. Tone of voice and body language are often important clues to how a person is feeling. Halting sentences, a set jaw, or an expression of bewilderment may say more about what a person is feeling than his words could convey.
- Control the urge to interrupt with a response. A nod of the head, a simple "yes" or "I understand" assures the speaker of your attention and encourages him to go on.
- If you do respond, reply with a simple "yes" rather than a "yes, but . . ." *But* is a word that signifies disagreement or at least qualification. It may discourage a speaker from going on or ensure that the speaker does not hear much after the word *but*. *Yes* is an affirmation and allows you to add your own qualifying remarks and still be heard.
- Remember you don't always have to respond immediately to a problem or a request. Even when a response is expected you may want to simply reply: "I'll get back to you later on this, after I've had a chance to think it over."
- Don't forget to thank the person who has taken time to talk with you even if he comes to vent or brings you a difficult problem. Remember the alternative: he could be grousing in the corridors or teachers' room instead of trusting you to hear him out.
- And finally, be patient with yourself and others who are not yet good listeners. Listening is an acquired skill. It takes practice.

3

Time Out for Reflection

Thought is action in rehearsal.

—Sigmund Freud

Why don't principals take Freud's reminder to heart? We work in a profession whose specific charge is to teach students the value of reflection as a prelude to action. Beyond the obvious fact that we should model what we teach, there are other compelling reasons for principals to schedule time for reflection.

To begin with, leaders are expected to have a vision, a mental map of where they aspire to lead people. Picture a field commander without a map and compass or a coach without a game plan. Principals, as leaders of their schools, must have an especially strong vision because schools are chaotic environments and the demands of multiple constituencies with different agendas will keep them that way. So, if school leaders are to pilot their schools through the turbulence of change, they will need a way of assessing at different points during the year where they are going and whether they are getting there.

Reflection is the way to do this assessment, so don't put it off. Schedule it right now, before your calendar fills up. Time for reflection is not a luxury that can be enjoyed at a principal's leisure; it is a basic requirement of leadership. If you arrive at school earlier than others to get prepared for the day, reflection can be part of that preparation. If you leave later than everyone else, make reflection part of your pre-departure routine. Occasionally schedule a solitary lunch and use part of that time for reflection. Leaders also need to schedule large chunks of time for group reflection. Sixty to ninety minutes a month is not too extravagant.

In one school where I worked, our entire leadership team scheduled a two-hour meeting once a month specifically for collective reflection. A few days prior to this meeting a team member would circulate an article from a professional journal or perhaps a chapter from a leadership book like this one for each of us to read and reflect on.

Everyone was expected to come prepared to discuss the article and its relationship to the challenges we faced, individually and collectively. Among the many benefits we derived from this activity was the chance to hear up close and personal the challenges that each individual faced, the frustrations he was feeling, as well as the triumphs and joys each of us was experiencing in our work life or personal life. This gave us more opportunity to better support one another and to celebrate each other's successes.

When you schedule a time to reflect, you will also need to choose a form of reflection. Choices range from personal and private to interpersonal and interactive reflection. Reflection can also be structured or informal. An informal approach to personal reflection might be keeping a journal. Writing is a particularly effective form of personal reflection since the act of putting something on paper compels you to bring clarity, precision, and coherence to your thinking.

A more structured approach (see sidebar) used individually or with a group can help you work through tough situations. Large group reflections are best done using a structured approach and a trained facilitator. Having a facilitator allows the leader to be part of the reflection group rather than leading it.

Once you've made your decision about the reflection process you are ready to confront the question, "What should I reflect upon?" If you choose to do a personal reflection, you might want to consider questions that define you as a person and a leader.

- Who am I and what do I stand for?

A REFLECTION PROTOCOL

1. Choose an incident to reflect on.
2. Spend five to ten minutes recalling the details of the incident.
3. Write down the precise details of what happened.
4. Describe the feelings you experienced during this incident.
5. Describe what you believe is the meaning of this incident—for you and others involved.
6. Describe what you learned from the incident and how it might influence you in the future.

Adapted from a protocol described by Simon Hole and Grace Hall McEntree in "Reflection Is at the Heart of Practice," *Educational Leadership*, May 1999.

- In what areas of my life or job do I find greater and lesser satisfaction?
- What are my strengths as a person? As a leader?
- What have I accomplished in my personal life? My professional life?

Consider personal questions first before moving on to broader questions relating to school, the community, and your role in them.

- Who are we and whom do we serve?
- What are the aims of our school?
- Are those aims broad enough, inclusive enough, inspiring enough?
- Which of our school practices further our aims; which inhibit them?
- Are we truly walking the talk we put into our mission and philosophy statements?
- Do we make daily decisions with our mission and philosophy firmly in mind?

It's easy to dismiss these kinds of questions as having already been answered, but to do so ignores the fact that as society changes, so do its needs, and schools have to change to meet those needs. As principal you need to check periodically to see which school practices are furthering the aims of the school's mission and philosophy and which are obstacles to achieving them.

Finally, you need time to reflect on both your successes and your failures. People often make the same mistakes over and over again, not because they are stupid but because they fail to reflect on the reasons for their mistakes and what they might do in the future to avoid them. Likewise, we do not learn from our successes simply by achieving them, but by reflecting on them. Ask yourself these questions:

- What obstacles did I or we have to overcome on the way to success?
- How did I or we confront them?
- What was the turning point?
- What resources did I or we find to support me or us?

Taking time out for thoughtful consideration is far better advice than the modern mantra of "Just do it." As responsible leaders, principals must take time to reflect on whether they should be doing "it" in the first place, how they should do it, and the probable effects of doing it. Then they will be better prepared to decide either to do it or drop it.

So as you prepare for the challenges of another school day, remember what Freud said and set aside some time for action's rehearsal. As a purposeful human being and responsible steward of your school, you need to cultivate quiet time for yourself to reflect. If you get used to doing that, you will gain the poise and confidence that come from knowing that you are well prepared for what you must do rather than merely ad-libbing another performance.

4

Principals Need to Stay Focused

Half a cup of coffee sits on my desk getting cold. The phone is ringing. My secretary pushes a fistful of purchase orders in front of me to sign. My computer blinks a reminder—*five minutes Leadership Team Meeting*. Outside my office a teacher paces back and forth, waiting to get in. Nestled among the miscellany of memos, mail, and phone messages is the "To Do List" I crafted last night. It's two hours into the school day and I haven't started on it yet. And there's the e-mail I haven't begun to read.

Last night as I was preparing my To Do List after the kind of day this one is shaping up to be and the day before was, I remembered how a teacher had told me that what he envied most about a principal's job was that: "You can close your door anytime and work undisturbed for an hour or more." Really, I thought, when was the last time any of us got to do that? The truth is that most principals have less control over their time than the teachers whose time they schedule. Herein lies a problem for principals who want to lead rather than merely manage.

To lead, as I mentioned in chapter 1, a principal must maintain a consistent focus on the goals he and his faculty are pursuing. Without that focus, he will be diverted from important leadership tasks by those ever-present urgent management ones. He will in effect become merely a manager rather than a leader.

In *Seven Habits of Highly Effective People*, Stephen Covey provides a yardstick for measuring the difference between a manager and a leader. Managers, he says, ask: "How can I accomplish certain things?" Leaders ask: "What are the things I want to accomplish?" Both questions are essential and both should be confronted. But, compelled by urgency, principals often fall into the habit of concentrating on the first question without ever considering the second.

Schools need good managers, but they need good leaders even more. We've all visited well-managed busy schools that give little thought to whether what they are trying to accomplish is of lasting value. These schools often have lofty-sounding mission statements; testimony that they once did reflect upon: "What do we want to accomplish?" But they have long since stopped examining for congruence between what they are doing and their stated mission.

For instance, many schools proclaim a commitment to the development of each child as a unique individual, and yet, *most* of their school practices favor standardization over individualization. A leader must be alert to such discrepancies, must make others aware of them, and with faculty, must address them.

We would be foolish to expect an institution as busy as a school which deals with many demands from multiple constituencies never to stray off course. Inevitably it will. It is the principal's job when this happens to make the proper moves to bring it back on course. Certainly, a principal cannot accomplish this by himself; he is after all only one member of a leadership team in the district. Nonetheless, if a principal takes the proper steps, the leadership team should support his efforts to get his school back on course. What are those steps?

I have said this before and I'll say it again because it is so vital to the success of what we hope to accomplish in schools. So write this down and keep it somewhere where it will be constantly before your own eyes. Everything we do in a school—all the courses we offer, all the extracurricular activities we run, all the field trips we take, all the plans we make—must be consistent with the mission and core values of the school. It is the things that are not consistent with these that are likely to lead a school astray. (See appendix 1 for an example of a school's mission statement and core values.)

In chapter 1, I compared focus to a bench vice that keeps a school anchored within the grip of what it should be doing. The two jaws of that bench vice are its mission and core values. These are so vital to the success of a school that if a school doesn't have them or has them but they aren't vibrant and inspirational and aren't directing what you and your faculty do daily, then your first step is to address this issue.

My purpose in this book is not to tell you how to develop a mission and core values so I'll assume you have them. If you don't, I mention a few resources at the end of this chapter that will help you get started in developing them. The point is that if you don't have them it will be mighty difficult, perhaps impossible, to keep your school focused.

If you have them, the next important step is to constantly keep them in view of your own eyes and the eyes of the school community. In schools I've served, one of my first actions was to have copies of the school's mission and core values printed, laminated, and put in every corridor, classroom, and meeting room. The reason for this is that, as school principal, it was my responsibility, as it is yours, to keep everyone focused on that mission and those core values by constantly referring to them and by constantly asking two questions when someone is proposing a new initiative.

The questions are:

1. How does this initiative help us further our school's mission?
2. What core value(s) does this initiative help us advance?

Remember mission and core values are the jaws of your focus bench vice.

How important are a school's mission and core values? As I matured into my role as a principal I learned always to ask whenever I interviewed for a new job about the school's mission and core values. If a school didn't have both or faculty, students, and parents couldn't tell me what they were, I knew it was going to be difficult to get that school focused, and I usually didn't take the job. Teachers, too, have gotten more sophisticated in interviews about asking questions that reveal a school's focus—or lack of it.

So you have your mission and core values and you've placed them where everyone in the school community can see them. Your next task, a never-ending one, I might add, is to be relentless about asking the two questions I mentioned. If teachers, board members, parents, and others cannot specifically identify how their proposed initiative will further the school's mission or values, you have to ask: "Then why are we even considering this?"

These two questions may stir some intense discussion as they did in one school where we considered what kinds of field trips would be approved. But if people in the school community get used to having to address these two questions, helping your school maintain its focus will be easier—not easy, just easier.

One more related item, and I'm borrowing this advice from advice given to writers: be willing to kill your own darlings. A principal can't just be merciless about nixing the ideas of others; he has to be particularly careful to be just as merciless with his own ideas. If he can't specifically detail how his planned initiatives further the mission and values of the school, he has to be willing to slay them, too. To do otherwise is to leave himself open to well-justified criticism.

Even if a principal can keep programs, proposals, and initiatives securely anchored within the jaws of the school's mission and core values, there's another factor of focus to be kept in mind. There are only so many things any school can accomplish in one year or in several years for that matter. You can't put ten pounds of apples in a five-pound bag no matter how appealing the apples or how good they may be for you.

A principal has to be hardnosed about how many goals and initiatives a school will have underway at any one time. Someone has to be hardnosed about that, and people expect the leader to be that someone. That means, by the way, that a principal may have to nix some of the good ideas of the PTA as well as his faculty and maybe even other members of the leadership team during a school year. But making those kinds of decisions is part of what makes leadership challenging and interesting.

Two other things I mentioned in previous chapters will help a principal keep the school focused. A leader must learn to remove himself from the cluttered urgency of the moment and consider whether what he and his staff are doing relates to what they believe they should be doing. This is the time for reflection that I mentioned a principal must build into his schedule. Second, in order to ensure focus, a smart principal plans backward from where he wants the school to be at the end of three to five years rather than just planning from one year to the next. In this way, a principal can make sure that school goals have continuity rather than being just a hodgepodge of yearly initiatives. I'll have more to say about this last point in the next two chapters.

I've made much of this idea of focus. I have even gone so far as to compare it to a bench vice and I mean every word I've said. But there is one final thing that a principal must keep in mind, and at first glance it may seem to contradict what I've already said. While staying focused and keeping others focused, a leader must remain open for the unexpected good idea or unexpected opportunity. Focused doesn't mean inflexible. You can even loosen a bench vice on occasion and then tighten it again.

5

Aylmer's Mistake and the Process of School Change

It is in the nature of man to be impatient with imperfection, to want to make things better—in fact to want to make them perfect. Overall, such impatience is a good thing; it has accounted for much of the progress we have made in improving the quality of human life and human institutions. But such impatience is not without its downside.

In 1846, Nathaniel Hawthorne published "The Birthmark" in his *Mosses from an Old Manse*. In this cautionary tale he described the efforts of Aylmer, a renowned alchemist, to remove a small birthmark from the cheek of his new bride Georgiana. She was widely acknowledged as a great beauty, but Aylmer was obsessed with removing the one slight flaw he saw in her otherwise perfect countenance. He succeeded. He removed the birthmark, but in the process killed his beloved Georgiana. There is a lesson, or should be, in this for those of us who wish to change what we see as imperfect—a lesson that I'd like to suggest applies to current school reform efforts.

To some reformers, schools appear infuriatingly slow and even implacably resistant to change. This can be intensely frustrating particularly for those from occupations that claim to survive by rapid adjustments to the ever-changing conditions in our world: politicians and businessmen come readily to mind. These reformers tend to become impatient, even churlish, with the pace of change in schools, forgetting perhaps that there are reasons for schools to be temperate and deliberate in their approach to change.

Schools, after all, are designed to be trustees of our historical, cultural, and intellectual past as well as guardians of our children's intellectual, emotional, and social growth—obligations, both of which can be easily compromised by thoughtless accelerated change. For these reasons and others that I will outline further on, schools better serve students and society with a more deliberate approach to change.

Consider this: In 1971, in *Future Shock*, Alvin Toffler wrote:

> Social rationality presupposes individual rationality. And this in turn, depends not only on certain biological equipment, but *on continuity, order and regularity in the environment.* It is premised on the correlation between the complexity of change and man's decisional capabilities. By blindly stepping up the rate of change, the level of novelty and the extent of choice, we are thoughtlessly tampering with the environmental conditions of rationality. (p. 367, *italics mine*)

Despite rhetoric to the contrary, schools and many other modern institutions are better served by change that seeks to preserve continuity, order, and regularity in their environment, even in the midst of change, than by rapid change that ignores the needs of that environment.

In saying this I am not advocating "sanctuary" or "executive privilege" from change for schools. Nor am I suggesting that the schools we have are perfect. We all know they are not. Like all institutions, schools must adapt and change to meet the demands of a changing future. But, the pace and processes we use to bring about that change will determine whether our changes will make schools better (however we choose to define that term) or merely push more and more of them onto the endangered species list. So what must we do to ensure that school change initiatives are salutary rather than pathogenic?

To begin, there is a ton of research literature detailing what we know about change and what has to be done to help people to successfully move through it; research literature that far too many change initiators choose to ignore.

No one can accomplish genuine change that involves human beings without a sound understanding of what people need to help them transition through change. No one! No one can effect genuine change without a plan for and a commitment to bringing people through this transition. No one! No one attempting to effect lasting change in education will be able to bring about that change without involving those who must make it work (teachers and principals) in the planning as well as the implementation process.

Such change requires *ownership* and you can't impose ownership on people. That is why state and federally mandated initiatives for school reform and even many plans initiated by school personnel themselves, which ignore the needs of people in the change processes, fail. As Robert Evans says in *The Human Side of School Change*:

> At the core of traditional approaches to change lies an arrogance that invites failure and plays a key role in the inability of those approaches to overcome resistance. Innovation is almost certain to encounter problems when implementation is defined according to only one reality [its creator's]. The reason

is straight-forward: the subjective reality of the implementer in schools, the personal experience of the teacher is crucial to successful innovation; transforming this subjective reality is a key task of change. When change agents assume they have "the right answer" and ignore the processes that foster this transformation they can be "as authoritarian as the staunchest defenders of the status quo." (p. 36)

Like it or not, those who propose change in schools must be willing to invest substantial time and energy into transforming the subjective realities of the people who must ultimately implement the changes; they must help them first to see the need for change and then provide them opportunity to adopt the change as their own. And in addition, a change advocate often has to invest an equal amount of time and energy into changing the subjective realities of parents and students who must come to believe in the value of the change. This commitment to working with people, not as we would wish them to be, but as they are now, at this moment in time and in this school, is one that many change agents have yet to make.

Without such a commitment, resistance will inevitably result and the initiative will fail, not because, as is often charged, school personnel failed to adapt to and adopt the change, but because the change agent failed to utilize processes that honor human nature. Worse still, a change initiative that fails to honor the needs of human beings can, and often does, poison the core of the school culture—that is, the relationship that exists between students, teachers, and the school leader. Here I have in mind the severe strain that the current brand of high-stakes testing worshiped by many state and federal authorities is placing on this relationship.

But, for those who have a desire to effect genuine change and who have the patience it takes to see change through to a satisfactory conclusion (or at least a willingness to work at developing that patience), here are a few suggestions:

- There are excellent books on the market that describe what must be done to accomplish change that lasts. Read at least one of them before you begin to initiate any substantive change. I'll recommend three here and you can find others in the bibliographies of these books: *The Human Side of School Change* by Robert Evans; *Managing Transitions: Making the Most of Change* by William Bridges; *Managing as a Performing Art: New Ideas for a World of Chaotic Change* by Peter Vaill.*
- Understand that all change is personal and idiosyncratic; change takes place on a person-to-person basis and what works in changing one

---

*I am indebted to the three authors whose books are mentioned herein for many of the suggestions that appear in this chapter.

person might not work with the next person. Take the time to find out what has deep meaning for individuals and what motivates each person or group of people you are working with. (It does not seem, for instance, to have occurred to many school reformers that incentives that motivate businesspeople [i.e., merit pay, career ladders] don't very often motivate teachers.)

- Truly appreciate that change involves loss of some kind, sometimes significant loss, and that we must help people deal with what they have lost if we want them to move on and adopt a proposed change.
- As much as possible involve the people who must make the change work in the planning as well as the implementation phase of the change. (This is often challenging in schools where the daily demands on teachers hinder their participation on committees and task forces that require a lot of extra time, but there are models for such participation that work.)
- Understand that when change occurs, people inevitably go through a period of confusion and loss of competence and confidence. This can be particularly painful for teachers who must face a classroom full of children each day—children who expect them to be competent and whose parents demand that they be. Have a plan for helping people move through this period of confusion and loss to a new stage of competence and confidence. Be patient and affirmative as people move into and through this phase.
- Know that when change takes place, some people gain power and influence while others lose what power they have. Be aware of who is gaining and who is losing and what effect that is having on them and on the proposed change.
- Often people have to be "unfrozen" from their current perception of reality and forced to face a new one. Learn how to do this without losing or destroying people in the process.
- Be realistic about changes you propose. Take into account the time, resources, and other demands of the job.

Bringing about change is a complex and intricate activity—much more so than most people have been led to believe by those who champion change. Change proposals, even very sound ones, often carry with them the specter of the Sword of Damocles. (Remember him? He was the courtier who talked so much about the *advantages* of being a king that King Dionysius seated him at a banquet underneath a sword hanging by a hair to demonstrate the *dangers* in a ruler's life.)

If our record of progress in the twentieth century has taught us anything, it should have taught us this: we can easily destroy good things in our effort to improve them. Hawthorne understood this. Aylmer didn't. Aylmer's impatience with imperfection blinded him to the Sword of Damocles perched above his own head and Georgiana's as well. In the end he suffered as a result of his ill-conceived improvement effort, but she suffered far more. Let's not repeat his mistake in our efforts to make schools better.

6

It's Time to Discipline School Reform

Embarking on school reform sometimes feels like spending an afternoon in an amusement park bumper car. Once underway, initiatives tend to careen out of control. One smacks into another and is in turn jolted from behind by yet another until they all get stalled in a tangled mess. Those involved in the initiatives end up fatigued and dispirited. "What will be different if we carry out this particular initiative?" was once a compelling question, but having been answered once, it is now forgotten in the flurry of activity that often results in reform gridlock.

The problem surfaces immediately at the beginning of the reform process. With enthusiasm at its height, reformers dash about trying to tackle every institutional shortcoming at once. Conventional wisdom holds that there is some logic behind adopting a broad brush approach; systematic change doesn't lend itself to pencil sketch correction. Nonetheless, overly ambitious efforts easily degenerate into an untidy sprawl of tatterdemalion activities that end up disabled and that exhaust, rather than satisfy, those who attempt them. The graveyard of failed school reform efforts is large and filled with many bones. Evans highlights the problem:

> Prioritizing is difficult, for people are reluctant to neglect any goals, no matter how difficult it is to address them all. In fact, most schools seem unable to concentrate their energies, or else they are not allowed to. Many are pursuing four, five, six initiatives at the same time. . . . The result is a press for what one principal calls "simultaneous multiple improvement." Wherever it occurs and whatever its mix, the result of simultaneous multiple improvement is almost invariably dispiriting (*The Human Side of School Change*, pp. 76–77).

Even when reformers within practice self-control, constituencies outside of schools may be pushing them into simultaneous multiple improvements.

> One of the reasons for overload and burnout is that there is a tremendous amount being thrown at teachers all at once these days. People in policy positions don't understand what it takes to achieve substantive change. So they keep throwing down one thing after another. I don't know any musician that simultaneously tries to learn to play every instrument in the orchestra. But that's what we're asking teachers to do. We're asking them to learn every instrument in the orchestra, and then we want them to go into the classroom and be the conductor. It's just not possible. It's almost like throwing a rock to a drowning person. Teachers are just beginning to feel skilled in a new practice and then Bang! a new idea, another curriculum, a new assessment, a new instructional model just when they are coming up for air. (Bennett cited in Brown & Cerylle, 1999, p. 66)

Clearly what the school reform movement now needs most is leaders strong enough to bring focus and discipline to it. If school reform is to endure and take root, its leaders must be more than merely visionary and messianic. They must be conservative in the sense that they are able to concentrate energy and resources around a few initiatives at a time—initiatives that are organic and interconnected.

Simultaneous multiple improvements loosely layered one over another, as we have discovered, are doomed. Systematic enduring change can be accomplished only by knitting together a few carefully selected reform initiatives that complement one another. In this way reform leaders ensure that changes are manageable and that those who must implement them have the training and resources to accomplish the task.

Today, much more so than in the past, leaders must have the courage to say *not yet* or even *no* to new reform initiatives that threaten to drain time and energy away from those currently underway. And they need to say *no* regardless of how powerful the constituency which proffers them might be. This is a formidable challenge, but it must be met if we are to get the reform car moving again. Changes that are viewed as evolutionary rather than revolutionary have a stronger success ratio.

It may be fashionable to speak on the floor of the Senate and in corporate training workshops of paradigm shifting change as if it were some totally new creation sprung from the head of Zeus, but the truth is that even paradigm shifting change tends to have an evolutionary history. Even where there is a radical leap to something new and unanticipated, a series of evolutionary steps has led us to the place where that leap can be made.

Change initiatives such as student-led parent-teacher conferences, for instance, evolve from teaching students to use rubrics and from teaching them to create and assess portfolios of their work. Student-led parent-teacher conferences may one day lead parents and teachers to agree that grades are not useful tools for reporting on student progress in learning. That would be revolutionary. But it would be evolutionary as well. Reform leaders should heed the lesson of the Mason jar.

A time management expert was conducting a session with a group of school leaders. She began by taking a Mason jar and placing it on a table. Then she took some lava rocks and placed them in the jar until they reached the rim.

Turning to the audience she asked: "Is this jar full?"

Someone answered: "Yes."

"Let's see," said the consultant taking a bucket of gravel and pouring it between the rocks. "Is it full now?"

By now some in the audience thought they were getting the point. "No!" offered one intrepid voice.

"Right," remarked the consultant as she took a bucket of fine sand and poured it between the gravel. "And now?"

"No!" shouted the audience getting into the spirit of things.

"Right again," said the consultant taking a pitcher of water and pouring it into the jar.

As the water drained between the recesses of sand, gravel, and stone, the consultant looked at her audience and inquired: "So what is the point of this little demonstration?"

One man replied confidently: "That no matter how full you think your schedule is you can always get more into it if you are organized and know how to manage your time."

"No, I'm sorry," said the consultant, "that is not the point of this demonstration. The point of this demonstration is that if you don't get the big things into the jar first, the truly important things, you won't be able to get them in later once the jar is full of less important things."

In many of our schools today the reform jar is so jammed with initiatives that the important things, the things that contribute most to student learning and growth, are barely distinguishable. With everything a priority there are no priorities, unless you consider relentless, uncompromising change the priority.

There is an old axiom that reads: "It takes nine months to have a baby no matter how many people you put on the job." Ours is an impatient age. We prefer to "get down and just do it." But there are things that demand a slower pace and rhythm than our frenetic bumper car approach. True,

schools must adjust and change like any other institution if they are to remain relevant and responsive to the changing needs of our society and its
children. But school leaders need to exercise more control over the changes
and bring more discipline to them, or they will not succeed.

Many of the reform initiatives now underway in schools are worthwhile
and can bring positive and enduring change. Individual school reform
movements can be a lighthouse for other schools which are attempting
similar educational reform. But only if we develop the discipline to prioritize our initiatives, focus them, and limit them to a manageable few upon
which we can build. Everyone enjoys the temporary chaos and excitement
of an occasional ride on those amusement park bumper cars. The confusion and collisions can be fun. But when it comes to school reform, we are
engaged in something more serious and enduring, aren't we?

7

Harried Principals Aren't Helpful Principals

Mahatma Gandhi once said, "There is more to life than increasing speed." The same might be said of work. But one would be hard pressed to believe that if he were today to peak into the office of most school principals. What would he see? A desk piled high with papers, the telephone ringing incessantly, forty or fifty e-mails screaming for attention from a computer monitor, a line of people queuing up outside the door, and a harried principal rushing from one task to another in a Herculean effort to stay on top of six or seven of them at once.

Most principals (I count myself among them, although I'm determined to learn how to change the pattern) have not yet learned you can't fit ten pounds of tasks into a five-pound day. Far from being the models of self-control, balance, and rationality they should be, many principals resemble butterflies on speed pills; they can't devote sustained attention to anything. And far from being oases of order and regularity that their schools need, the principals' offices and their staffs manifest the frenzy you'd expect to find on the floor of the New York Stock Exchange. One can only hope that the principal's office is not a mirror of what is happening in the rest of the school. But it often is.

Stop! A harried leader is not a helpful leader. And schools need calm, well-balanced, helpful leaders every bit as much as they need visionary ones. In fact, in this era of frenetic change in schools, principals should be devoting at least as much time to helping teachers to be more focused and less frantic as they are to formulating new visions for the school or embarking on new improvement initiatives.

As Andy Hargreaves and Michael Fullan point out in *What's Worth Fighting For Out There* (1998), overeager teachers and their leaders can easily fall into the trap of *projectites*—"pursuing change frantically through one uncompleted task after another" (p. 109). In such schools teachers, principals, students, and parents end up feeling frustrated rather than fulfilled, angry rather than empowered. Harried principals can never be part of the solution, they can only add to the problem. The good news is that a harried principal can choose to change. But where does he begin?

A principal who undertakes the task of becoming a more well-balanced helpful leader begins by learning to better order, regulate, and control the pace of his own day. A principal who can't do this can't help others regulate and control theirs. But how can a principal gain control of his own chaotic existence?

First, by making a commitment to gaining such control. Gaining better control of your own schedule means committing to the task as though it was the first and most important improvement initiative you have. For some of us, it should be.

The second step is to establish your priorities. What is it you want to accomplish for the year, the semester, the quarter, the week, and today? Work backward in that order so that your important priorities don't get nickeled and dimed to death by the urgent (but not necessarily important) demands of each day.

Your priorities, once established, should be a rudder by which you steer the course of your workdays. Write down your priorities (yearly goals if you want to call them that) and keep them where you can see them. Revisit them frequently assessing your progress on each. Don't allow yourself, or others, to forget them. Publish them to your staff, your head of school, and your fellow administrators. Once they know your priorities, they know how you are expecting to spend the majority of your time.

Third, plan out the work you must accomplish on your priorities in big chunks: year, months, and weeks. Put a timeline on each chunk of work. Write down the resources you'll need (human and material) to help you get the job done. This is often called *action planning*. Here is a simple action plan template:

- Objective
- Action steps
- Resources needed
- Person(s) responsible
- Completion date
- Evidence of completion

Fourth, work to develop patience and perseverance in pursuit of accomplishing your priorities. On the bulletin board in front of my desk is a poster that reads: "Great works are achieved not by strength but by perseverance"—Samuel Johnson. It serves as a constant reminder to me that nothing truly significant or lasting is ever accomplished in the absence of the companion virtues of patience and perseverance.

Whenever I reviewed what my faculty and I had achieved together over the years, as I often did in preparation for our first faculty meeting of the year, I found that most of our goals were not accomplished in the year we developed them. They were accomplished a year later, or even the year after that. And they were accomplished when we had the patience to persevere despite changes in our faculty and central administration and in the face of numerous other hurdles.

Cultivate patience and perseverance at work and away from it. Anyone can lead when the task is easy and the chances for success inevitable; real leaders emerge when the task is difficult, seemingly impossible, and the road ahead is obscured in fog.

Fifth, develop strategies for dumping some of the extra baggage that eats away at the time you need for pursuing your leadership priorities. There is a lot of jetsam in the cargo of any leader; it needs to be sorted out from time to time and thrown overboard. Successful leaders stay focused on the big picture priorities and don't allow themselves to be distracted by other claims on their attention. Learn to jettison at least some of the excess baggage in your work life: meetings that have little or nothing to do with what you must accomplish, committees that want an administrator as window dressing, and tasks that could and should be done by others.

No one will encourage or help you eliminate the excess from your schedule. This is a ruthless task that must be done by you, and it takes courage because everyone who makes a claim on your time believes that claim should be your priority. Here the eleventh commandment of administration can prove helpful to you if used judiciously: *It is a lot easier to ask for forgiveness than permission.* "I'm sorry I had to miss that meeting because—," "I'm going to have to withdraw from this committee because—." Of course, it is far better if you can avoid taking on excess baggage rather than to have to jettison it once it is in your schedule.

There is more to life than speed and excess. Want to be a less harried, more helpful, and more successful leader? Develop focus, patience, and perseverance. Add to them balance, optimism, enthusiasm, and joy. There you have it; the formula for success whatever your personal limitations or the circumstances of your current environment. Need inspiration? Consider this.

Erik Weihermayer is thirty-two years old. He has worked as a middle school teacher, run marathons, and performed skydiving acrobatics. He is a downhill skier, scuba diver, and long distance cyclist. And he has been blind since age thirteen. Recently, he became the first blind climber to reach the top of Mount Everest.

When he was interviewed by a CNN reporter after the Everest climb, Erik offered this comment which should serve as good advice for all of us who are pursuing our own great goals. "Be focused. Be full of energy. Keep relaxed. Don't let all those distractions—the fear and doubt—creep into your brain, because that's what ruins you up there" (*Bits and Pieces*, August 9, 2001). Erik doesn't accomplish his goals by being faster and busier than other people. He accomplishes them by being more focused and determined. There is more to life than speed.

8

So You're the Principal; Well, What Have You Done for Yourself Today?

One afternoon I opened the door to a school storeroom and knew immediately something odd was happening in there. The lights were out and it was very dark inside. That's not unusual for a storeroom. But I could hear the sound of breathing and of a radio playing very softly. When I flicked on the lights I startled a custodian who was catnapping on a hammock jerry-rigged between a battered old teacher's desk and an office chair. He was a bit embarrassed as I was. I said "Hello, how's it going?" got what I was looking for, and left him lying there, wondering, I'm sure, what I was thinking.

He couldn't possibly have imagined what I was thinking as I walked back to my office.

So you're the principal! Well, what have you done for yourself today? You spend your days trying to keep pace with e-mails, memos, paperwork, and "got a minutes." You go to meetings, monitor the corridors and cafeteria, and visit classes. But what have you done for yourself today?

It sounded like a selfish question because I, of course, like other principals have been trained to think of everyone else first. But was it really? Is it selfishness or sanity that suggests we principals need to treat that question seriously? Evidence abounds that principals who don't attend to their own needs are not as able to attend to the needs of others. In *Managing Transitions* William Bridges writes:

> The average manager's situation at home and at work is made up of constant and difficult change. It often seems like something between a Greek tragedy and a sitcom. No wonder most managers spend a great deal of time wondering if it is all worth it. And it is understandable if you are wondering . . . How do you take care of yourself? (1991, p. 88)

That custodian knew he had to take care of himself; and he knew he needed to recoup the energy he'd expended in a full morning of hard work. He wasn't a sluggard; he had a reputation as a good worker. I wondered if I might learn a lesson from him. The work we principals do besides being terribly important is enormously exacting. "Depleting" is the word that Roland Barth uses in *Improving Schools from Within* (1991). Barth, a former principal, issues a warning to all of us still in the field whose Spartan work ethic keeps us from taking care of ourselves. "The bottom line is that the work life of a school principal is depleting. Depletion of leadership leads to depletion of faculty, of school, of community and ultimately of the learning experience of the students" (p. 66).

Barth quotes a Michigan principal who sums up our situation well: "It isn't the mountains that exhaust me; it's the pebbles in my shoe." Once exhausted, I ask you: of what value are we to those in our school, in our home, and in our community?

So, let's say you're convinced and determined to do something about taking better care of yourself. What are you going to do, set up a hammock in your office and take afternoon naps? Not likely! But, here are a few things you might consider. *No*, just thinking about them isn't enough. When you finish this chapter, pick a few of these ideas, write them down, and put them where you can see them. Review them once a day to assess how you are doing on them. (You see some of the things we've learned in assessment workshops can help us in our own personal lives if we're willing to apply them there, too.)

Eat a healthy breakfast and lunch. How many lunches have you missed lately? Well, stop that right away. It isn't just students and teachers who need fuel to keep going, principals do, too. Are you trying to thrive on caffeine and nicotine? Well, get control of that as well. Too much of either isn't good for you. But you already know that. Write down on your daily calendar the time you will go to lunch. If you still find you are missing lunch despite this reminder, share the time with your secretary who will insist that you keep this lunch appointment. And if you find that even this doesn't work, start making arrangements to go to lunch with one or two other people.

The point is to break the habit of not going to lunch by establishing the habit of going. Don't teachers report students who habitually miss lunch? How would it look if a concerned teacher or secretary or nurse reported you for missing lunch?

Learn to leave the job each day at a reasonable hour. A Japanese friend told me that Japanese middle managers are expected to stay at work until the boss decides to leave. That keeps many of them at their desks manufacturing bogus work long after they could have called it a day. What a silly activity! What lack of regard for the value of personal and family life! We need not emulate it.

And yet, I suspect that many of us do, unaware that we are setting a bad example for teachers and support staff. Even if they don't attempt to match our marathon work hours, they leave for home knowing that while the principal may preach about the value of family life, he doesn't practice what he preaches. And let us not fool ourselves: such hypocrisy doesn't escape the notice of our students and their parents.

Take daily breaks. Remember the custodian I mentioned. He knows the value of taking a break. Why don't we? What is it that keeps the principal from taking a break during the day? Most of the time, the answer is . . . the principal. If our workdays always feel like we are making love to a gorilla, we need to take a good look at ourselves when we ask: *why?*

Here is a technique I've used to build a break into most days before things get crazy. I begin by keeping a weekly calendar on my computer which both my secretary and I can access. Every weekend I review the calendar to see what's coming up. I look for open time slots, and in some of these I write in "time for observation" or "time for walking around." Built into these times is time for me to take a break. What do I do during these times? I do some professional reading, journaling, I have a snack, or I just kick back and relax for a few minutes.

Develop some friendships with people who aren't part of the job. I often hear principals, myself included, complaining about the fact that all we ever talk about is school. Here again, I wonder if we're not responsible for mixing the cyanide we drink. There are plenty of people out there who have other things on their mind besides education. Are you making an effort to talk with them? Or are your friends all educators? What about the person who sells you that cup of coffee in the morning? The one who gases up your car or rents you a video? There are opportunities there to talk about things other than school.

In my last job before going overseas, I struck up a friendship with the woman who managed the local video store. Whenever I came in, we'd engage in witty repartee with one another—much to my delight, hers, and not a few of the other customers. It was a great way to relieve the stress of a busy week. Phyllis and I had our own system of rating films. When I returned a film she and I had seen, we'd present one another with a chocolate kiss if we liked it. And if we didn't? A dog biscuit. I enjoyed my chats with Phyllis as much as I enjoyed any film I rented from her.

Make time for exercise and other activities. As school leaders we battle with the determination of a bear protecting her cubs to preserve arts, physical education, and field trip opportunities for our students. Why? Because we know they are essentials of a well-balanced life. What about us? How many of us take time to engage in these same activities?

My brother-in-law, who runs daily after work, says that the answers to the most difficult and perplexing problems of his job often come to him when he's relaxed and out running. I found the same thing. I also write for relaxation. I know other principals who play musical instruments, sing in a choir, are part of an exercise group or a community theater group, or join book discussion groups. There are plenty of opportunities for exercise and for other forms of relaxation outside of school. So read a book, learn to play a musical instrument (or at least listen to music), take a hike with the family, go for a run, or go fishing.

Take mini-sabbaticals. Let's face it: sabbaticals for principals are an impractical artifact from the past. How many of us can afford to wait seven years before we are eligible to take a break to renew ourselves? And even if we last that long in one job, how many school boards are willing to give a principal a one-year hiatus?

We would be better served by consigning the seven-year sabbatical to a museum with the other dinosaurs and looking for opportunities to take mini-sabbaticals—retreats away from the daily routine of the job that last anywhere from a few days to a few weeks. These might take the form of attendance at workshops or principal's institutes, temporary job exchanges, visits to other schools, joining a school accreditation team, visits to recruiting fairs, or simply taking some time off to relax and regain our energy.

In "Birches," Robert Frost, describing his need to retreat temporarily from the demands of daily life, wrote: "I'd like to get away from earth a while. And then come back to it and begin over. . . . That would be good both going and coming back" (p. 31). A slight twist of Frost's words yields an excellent prescription for what ails every principal once in a while. "I'd like to get away from *school* a while. And then come back to it and begin over again."

That would be good both going and coming back. There is nothing to be ashamed of in admitting we need an occasional break from the rigors of our work to renew our energy and spirit or in taking steps to address that need. If we principals want to be taken seriously as stewards of the health and well-being of our students and staff, we must first establish credibility with them by being responsible stewards of our own.

9

They Never Told Me
That in Principal's School!

A retiring principal, a veteran of many campaigns, was cleaning out his desk for the last time and talking with his replacement. They had spent several weeks together as part of the transition plan and the veteran had exhausted the time he had to give advice to his eager young replacement.

"Well," he said, "I've told you all I have to tell you at the moment, and it's time to go. But listen, you're bound to get yourself into a few jams from time to time; we all do. So I've prepared three 3 × 5 note cards of advice for you for when I'm not here. They are numbered. Use them in the order I've given them. I've put them here in this little metal box. Take it and put it where you can find it when you need it." And with that he departed.

Things went on swimmingly for the new principal for a while. But, as predicted, within six months he found himself in an impossible situation. He struggled mightily with himself for a while trying to find a solution. But to no avail. And then, just when it seemed that everything would be lost, he remembered the metal box. He rushed to where he had left it, opened it, took out the first 3 × 5 card, and turned it over.

"Blame me!" it stated simply.

At the next faculty meeting the principal rose and declared: "It is not fair to hold me responsible for the errors of my predecessor. But together I'm sure we can move beyond him and find a solution for this problem." His predecessor's advice worked like a charm.

Things went well for a while before the new principal again found himself in an unforgiving situation. He remembered the metal box and rushed to it for relief. Once more he was rewarded.

"Form a committee," he read.

At the next meeting of the school board, he stepped to the microphone and confidently proposed: "What we need in this situation is a committee to conduct a study and make some recommendations." It worked like a charm and he was again free from anxiety.

It took a year and a half before he found himself in another impossible situation. By now he was experienced enough to know he shouldn't wait when things were bad. So he rushed off to get relief from the little metal box. Opening the box he turned over the last of the 3 × 5 cards.

"Update your résumé."

Now I'm in the position of that honored ancient I mentioned—retired and sharing some of the experience I've gleaned over many seasons as a principal. My suggestions may be neither as succinct nor as astonishing as the retiring principal's but I trust they will be helpful. I never received this advice in courses and seminars I took while preparing to be a principal. I often find myself wondering why they weren't included. These are things I've had to learn by experience over the years. I must, therefore, assume full responsibility, along with those who use it, for the results of this advice. I hope it will serve you well.

RESPONSIBILITY VERSUS POWER

Experienced principals know that their jobs are much more heavily weighted toward responsibility than power. When they hear someone talking about "the power" of the principal all the time, they know he is either a new principal or, more than likely, not a principal at all. When I was a novice principal just cutting my teeth on the job, I had a power proverb I reserved for those who were particularly irritating in their opposition to decisions I made. It went like this: "If you want to get into a pissin' contest with me, you'd better come with a heavy raincoat and a big umbrella."

After a couple of decades in the job, I learned that I was the one who'd better have an umbrella and raincoat on hand. There is power in the principalship, to be sure, but that power usually resides in the opportunity to persuade rather than push. It turns out a principal is much better served by broad shoulders than by burly biceps.

DON'T COME RUNNING WITH A FIRE HOSE
EVERY TIME SOMEONE SHOUTS "FIRE!"

A principal soon learns that overreaction is every bit as dangerous as underreaction. When there is a problem, people expect action from the principal, and a principal is always primed for action. Therein is the problem. If a principal does not take adequate time to assess a problem, he can rush out in full battle gear to confront a blazing inferno that is not there and never was. That is not only embarrassing, it is often counterproductive, giving credence to and creating anxiety about a mythical catastrophe.

Overreaction often occurs when someone, could be a faculty member, a parent, or a student, comes into the principal's office upset about something, vents his or her spleen, and announces that there are a whole lot of others out there who feel the same way. The experienced principal who takes the time to properly assess the situation before rushing out to confront the so-called "inferno" often finds that the sulfur his informant smelled and the heat he felt was nothing more than the flame of his own ignited anger. As a principal you will encounter many who light a match and are convinced they've set the woods on fire. Be forewarned and be deliberate in your response.

BOUNDARY SETTING OR "MY DOOR ISN'T ALWAYS OPEN"

I don't know who it was who first announced "My door is always open," but you can be sure he didn't get much work done after that. Well meaning though that advice was meant to be, it is nonetheless bad advice. If the principal's door is always open, one can be certain that, like a gully in a torrential rainstorm, there will always be a steady stream flowing through it and much of the important business of the school will be inundated by the flood.

If a doctor's door was always open, we would never see him in the hospital and he would perform no operations. If a lawyer's door was always open, none of his cases would ever come to court. And if a priest's door was always open, an impatient and irritated congregation would be left waiting in church for a service that would never begin. A far better motto for principals to adopt is: "I will always make myself available to you if you have a need." That gives a principal time and opportunity to assess and prioritize needs and to allot his time judiciously.

And while we are on this subject a principal needs to know how to set another boundary as well. When a principal goes home for the day, he becomes a private citizen: a parent, a spouse, or a good neighbor with obligations other than school. At those times office hours should be over for anything other than emergencies. And when a principal attends a school function as a parent rather than as a principal, others need to learn to respect that boundary as well and to reserve their needs for another time, except of course in the cases of emergencies.

Principals need to establish these boundaries for their own health and welfare and for the health and welfare of their family. Where there are no clearly identified boundaries, there are no boundaries. One of the things we principals should be taught in principal's school is the polite but important art of demurring: "I'll be in school tomorrow from __ to __. Could you contact me about that then?" To be a genuine leader a principal must be a servant to those he leads, but never a slave. The two are not the same and the effective principal learns to recognize the difference.

Finally, no matter how effective a principal may be, there comes a time when he must recognize it's time to utilize that final 3 × 5 card. Either for his own growth and development or for the growth and development of the students, teachers, and community members he serves. There is no reproach in this; only opportunity for renewal.

10

A Reality Check for
a New School Leader

When I left the teaching ranks to become an administrator I was astonished at how quickly teachers who had previously bonded with me, in what we both believed was to be a solid friendship, abandoned me. My first experience with that reality came when, as assistant principal, I assigned a basketball buddy of mine to cover a homeroom. I thought of it as a minor duty assignment; he did not. He promptly announced to other faculty members that I had crossed over "to the other side"; I was "an administrator." The way he said *administrator* left no doubt he viewed me, and other administrators, with as much respect as he had for head lice.

A lot of literature suggests to neophyte administrators that they can bridge the divide between faculty and administrators by following a few simple rules that will result in teachers honoring and loving them. The simple rules usually go something like this: Treat everyone like you'd like them to treat you, show no favoritism, and be open and honest with everyone in all your dealings with them. My experience with such simple formulas for leadership success is that they are more simplistic than simple, and administrators would do well not to trust the warranty that comes with them.

Let me be clear from the outset that I'm not saying not to treat everyone as you'd want to be treated or not to be honest and open, and I'm not promoting favoritism. What I am saying is that practicing these rules is not as simple as it sounds. There are times, for instance, when you have information that you simply can't share openly and candidly for one reason or another. And even when you do practice the simple rules of leadership success (I wasn't showing favoritism when I assigned my basketball buddy to a homeroom), there is no guarantee that you'll be successful in getting understanding, let alone affection. Human beings are more understanding and affectionate when they get what they want.

There is a gulf between administrators and teachers that is difficult to bridge. From my experience those who have the most reluctance to bridge it are teachers rather than administrators. This is not a knock on teachers but an admonition to acknowledge one of the simple realities of our humanity. It's difficult to understand someone else's situation unless you've walked in their shoes. And while empathy is a great quality, and highly to be sought after, it's usually harder to find than short pants in a New England winter, especially if you are a school leader or any leader for that matter. Most people expect a leader to empathize with them, not the other way around.

Most administrators I know have been teachers but very few teachers have been administrators. This makes it easier for administrators to understand what teachers do, feel, and need than it is for teachers to recognize what a principal feels and needs, or even in many cases, what he actually does.

Let me try to illustrate this with a simple analogy. I want to be careful with this analogy because in using it I'm not suggesting that teachers are immature, only that they have never been in the same situation as administrators.

When I taught point of view as a high school English teacher I'd often remind students who felt that adults "don't understand kids" that, while there was always a possibility that that was true, they should keep one important fact in mind. "Every adult has been fifteen, sixteen, and seventeen years old and has had experience with what it's like to think, feel, and act like a teenager (even if you believe they've forgotten a lot of that). On the other hand, no teenager has experienced how he or she will think, feel, and act when he or she is twenty-five, thirty, forty, or older." Some kids could relate to that idea, many could not.

So where am I headed with this? What does it mean for principals? It doesn't mean that they should give up in their efforts to gain faculty understanding and support. It doesn't mean that school leaders should stop reading leadership books or trying to put into practice what they read in them. It does mean that all of us in leadership positions should remember what Christ tried to teach the leaders of the Hebrew church: there is a difference between the letter of the law and the spirit of the law, and it is with the spirit of the principle that we need to be concerned.

What that means for school leaders is that we will have to have the courage to accept the reality that when we actually put into practice the spirit of an important principle of leadership like showing no favoritism, some faculty may view us as violating that principle.

Secondly, as school leaders, principals are far better served by settling for respect rather than looking for love and admiration. Even at that, respect may come grudgingly and only after the fact. Many of the best compliments

I've had from faculty about my leadership have come after they've left the school in which I was serving as principal, or I've left and they were serving under a new administration.

Perhaps the greatest obstacle to building a bridge to understanding between faculty and administration is, as I've previously noted, faculty misperception of an administrator's power. Many people believe that administrators have much more power than they actually have and have little understanding of how much responsibility administrators have. You can usually tell the difference between those who do understand and those who don't. The ones who don't are always making references to your "power." The ones who do simply say: "Boy, I wouldn't want your job!"

More has to be done to educate faculty members about the responsibilities and demands of school leadership positions. How to do that and who should do it would be a good subject for discussion among school leaders and a good topic for another book. (See suggestions in this chapter.) Until that education has been successfully accomplished, I recommend that new school leaders not get caught up in Kojac's favorite expression "Who loves you, baby?" and spend their time concentrating on doing their jobs and doing them well. If you do that, to paraphrase an old expression, respect, and maybe even love, will find its way.

SUGGESTIONS

- There is a lot of literature about the responsibility of leadership. But what about the responsibility of followership; some discussion and some articles about that would be an important addition to the professional Library.
- Teachers who get to shadow a school leader for a day or longer usually gain a better appreciation for what he does. Usually those who shadow a leader are only the ones who want someday to be one. Perhaps there would be some benefit in giving all teachers a chance to shadow a school leader.
- When you have to leave the building for hours or days, ask a teacher to be acting principal for the time you are gone. I've done this on numerous occasions. The results have been mixed and interesting. In some instances, the teacher appreciated the experience; in others, the teacher asked me never to ask him to do that again. In every instance, the acting principal got a better understanding of what a principal's job was like.

11

"Say Something Nice to Me": A Strategy for Dealing with the Chronically Cranky

I'll admit it. I have little patience with chronic complainers. I endure the dreary moments I'm compelled by duty, or by compassion, to be with them, but I spend most of that time silently wishing they were gone and trying to figure out an unobtrusive way to get rid of them. You know the type: look-a-likes of that couple in *American Gothic*.

They come at you, their faces pinched with anxiety, their entire aura a cloud of concern. For them the glass is always half empty and continually leaking through a thousand little pinholes. I picture them rising gloomily in the morning and proceeding through the day tormented by discontent before finally retiring to bed burdened and disgruntled.

I'm a school administrator, a trained service provider, and I feel guilty when I just want to get rid of someone. I know those who come through my door aren't always right in the criticism they offer. Nevertheless, I'm disposed to listen to them as if they might be.

Still, I find the chronically cranky visitor, whether he or she be a teacher, a parent, or a community member, a challenge. It's difficult to sit there smiling gravely (the one smile they seem to appreciate), listening for something I can build on as moment by moment they add to the fatigue of my day. These are needy people, and what they need most is to see at least a little of life's sunshine. They need to be tutored to see "the glass as half full." And they can be. Here are a couple of examples to illustrate my point: one from popular culture and one from my professional experience.

In the movie *As Good As It Gets* (a title that fits nicely with the glass is half full metaphor) Jack Nicholson plays a cynical sourpuss who has everything (except friends) and who is constantly complaining about minutiae. Helen

Hunt plays a single working mother struggling to make ends meet while trying to attend to her severely asthmatic son.

Nicholson is attracted to her because she is always upbeat and optimistic despite her circumstances. In a pivotal scene that marks a dramatic change in their relationship, Hunt interrupts one of Nicholson's diatribes of discontent with the words: "Say something nice to me; I need to hear you say something nice to me." It's a struggle for the Nicholson character; he hasn't had much practice, but he finally chokes out that wonderful line: "You make me want to be a better man." And after that, he is a better man.

When we are able to activate those positive endorphins, neurons, or whatever they are, that exist in all of us, something remarkable happens. Positive thinking really does cleanse the mind and spirit of toxins of discontent and discouragement.

Several years ago I was working in a school that went from placing students with special needs in substantially separate classrooms to mainstreaming them with support in the regular classroom. During the first year of the new model, my assistant principal and I met every two weeks with the teachers collaborating within this new model. We wanted to hear what problems they were encountering and how the program was progressing. By the way, note the order of priorities in that last sentence; it's important for what follows.

Week after week we encountered a litany of complaints about the program. Following one of these sessions, tired and beaten, I said: "I can't take much more of this negativity, Jan; maybe we should just give it up!" Jan suggested we try a different stratagem at our next meeting.

We began that next meeting by asking each participant to identify one success he or she had had within the program in the past week. The result was transformative. We went from meetings chronicling frustration after frustration to meetings where descriptions of accomplishments empowered people to believe that together we could overcome any obstacle that stood in the way of the model's success.

We had planned to devote just ten minutes to accentuating the positive in the hope of alleviating the negative. Instead, the group devoted an hour to achievements and twenty minutes to problems that needed to be remedied. And all left satisfied. The simple stratagem of talking first about what was working helped people to see the glass as half full instead of half empty and helped them believe that we had the power to go out and find a fountain to fill it up the rest of the way.

Human beings are naturally inclined to look for problems that need to be solved and to be impatient when a solution is not immediately forthcoming. There is an upside to this, particularly when it is tempered with perspective; it ensures our continued growth and progress. But there is a downside as well. When this inclination isn't tempered by perspective, it can result in chronic crankiness and complaining.

No one relishes being accosted by Spiro Agnew's "nabobs of negativity." It is easy to understand why we spend our time trying to avoid them. But avoidance isn't always an effective strategy or even an available option. In all likelihood, the complainers will be back. Perhaps it's time to try a more transformative strategy, one that may prove more satisfying for both you and your cranky visitor.

The next time someone approaches your office shrouded in clouds of gloom, usher him in and get him comfortable. And then in a style uniquely your own, start the conversation with: "Say something nice to me."

12

Principals Must
Avoid Doggy Behavior

I took my daughter's dog for a walk the other day. As often happens when I take Max for his walk, it turned out to be less a walk and more a series of stops and re-starts. Max had to sniff out every trace of other dogs' scent and cover it up with his own. While Max returned home satisfied, I did not. The walk left me frustrated. It reminded me of what some principals feel the urge to do when they take over as the new leader of a school; they run around like a hound in heat trying to cover up any scent left by the previous administration.

I have felt that urge; I admit it. It's a bad idea. There are better ways to leave a leadership mark that are less piddling and more permanent. With that in mind, here are some suggestions that will help you avoid doggy behavior.

TAKE TIME TO HONOR THE PAST

Every school, even one that needs change, has a history of accomplishments. Those accomplishments may be hidden deep in the display case of failure, back behind all those trophies of non-accomplishment, but they are there. Take time to find them, polish them up, and bring them forward. They are something to build on. Here's one way to remind people of these accomplishments.

Schedule a Faculty Celebration

Before school opens for students in the fall is a great time to do this. Announce to all staff (not just teachers) that during this time, "We will be honoring the past and I'd like all of you to be present."

Review the history of the school by decades. Begin with those staff who have been at the school the longest, for instance those who have been at the school thirty years or longer. Ask a member (or members) of each decade to address two questions. What were the challenges the school staff faced during that decade? What were the major accomplishments of the school during that decade? Be patient. Allow time for whoever wants to speak, but keep everyone focused on the two questions.

When the members of one decade have finished have them remain standing (or sitting) center stage and ask everyone else to acknowledge them with applause. Then call the members of the next decade forward to address the same two questions. You will need a space big enough for all members of your staff to be standing or sitting center stage by the conclusion of this activity. Go decade by decade right down to the latest decade.

Once the veteran staff members have all been gathered center stage, have the new staff, including you, join them and speak to these two questions. Why did I want to become a member of *this* school? What are my best hopes for this school year? When everyone is done speaking invite the staff to congratulate one another by shaking hands and embracing. Then break for coffee so that the good feelings can continue before you get down to the business part of your agenda.

Scheduling an activity like this accomplishes two important things. First, it activates those positive endorphins that give everyone energy and enthusiasm for facing the tasks ahead. We spend so much time in schools talking about what has to be fixed that we often exhaust ourselves with dissatisfaction. Robert Browning asked: "A man's reach should exceed his grasp, else what's a heaven for?" (Auden and Pearson, p. 155). Everyone occasionally needs to be reminded that the perfection we strive for will always be elusive; so let's learn to enjoy the striving.

The second thing this activity does is it sends a message to everyone that you recognize that you are not standing on the neck of your predecessor but on his shoulders as you and the school community work to bring the school to its next level of achievement. We are so future focused as a culture that we often forget the accomplishments of our predecessors—accomplishments without which we'd have no foundation to build on. One of the functions of school is to remind people of the importance of history. One of yours as a leader is to remind the school community of the importance of its history.

ACCENTUATE THE POSITIVE

Remember that old song that said we need to "accentuate the positive and eliminate the negative"? Well it's good advice particularly in schools where we spend so much time trying to correct error—our own as well as our students'. I'm by no means promoting being a Pollyanna, but in truth, there are far more Chicken Littles in the world (and the school world) than Pollyannas.

Former Speaker of the House Sam Rayburn used to remind freshman Congressmen: "Any old jackass can kick down a barn, but it takes a carpenter to build one" (Rayburn). You may or may not be a freshman administrator, but your job is to be a carpenter.

Structure discussions with people in your new school so that they tell you what is working before they get into what isn't. This may call for some strategy on your part especially when you are talking with people who aren't used to recognizing what's working. Remember Jack Nicholson's character in *As Good As It Gets?* Keep at it. You may not succeed in making a pessimist want to be a better man (or woman) but you may broaden the scope of his or her seeing. And if you don't, you will at least broaden your own as you gather information not just on what you have to build but what you have to build on.

I've seen the antithesis of this strategy used, and it was a disaster. A consultant, undoubtedly pressed for time (he knew better, I'm certain), gathered representatives of a school community together for a school improvement session. He began the session by asking the group to identify what was wrong with the school and needed to be fixed. By the end of the three-hour session people were so angry with one another (and with him) and so dissipated by despair I had to wonder if they'd ever recover enough to fix any of the problems they catalogued.

SPEAK WELL OF YOUR PREDECESSOR

And finally this. Speak well of your predecessor; or, if you can't, don't speak of him at all. Very few people admire people who tear others down. They may agree with them, may even think the victim deserves the criticism, but they seldom admire the assassin. Remember your mother's advice: "If you can't say something nice about somebody, don't say anything at all."

Usually, you can find good things to say about your predecessor. So say them. You don't have to trumpet his name from the rooftops, but do acknowledge the contributions he made whenever you can.

I remember replacing a principal who had virtually been run out of town by a group of disgruntled parents and teachers. Listening to them, you would have thought the guy was a serial killer. He wasn't. He had accomplished many things in that school, things that had been forgotten over the years, things I had opportunity to build on and occasion to comment on.

Others were eventually able to remember his contributions and appreciate and acknowledge them.

Even dog lovers don't enjoy watching their canines scampering about attempting to cover up the scent of anything that has ever walked that way before them; it's foolish behavior. Those who take over a new leadership should avoid such behavior. It's for the dogs; leave it with them.

13

The Courage of Educational Leaders

One quality we don't hear discussed much in conversations about educational leadership is courage. Oh sure, it's mentioned in passing on the list of leadership characteristics, but few who write or speak about educational leadership dwell on it or on why leaders need it and in how many areas they will be called upon to use it. That's a significant oversight. If there ever was a profession where leaders need to exercise courage forcefully and frequently, it is education.

Yet, if you listen to most conversations about educational leadership, you are left with the impression that while courage is required of warriors, athletes, corporate leaders, and an occasional politician, education is too dandified a profession to require it of its leaders. How absurd! Can anyone imagine a principal or superintendent getting through a month, let alone a year, without having to face multiple challenges that demand courage?

Now more than ever schools are battlegrounds on which society contests its shifting social beliefs and attempts to sort out its enduring social dilemmas. What kind of education do we want for our children? Should we allow discussion of religion or values in school? Should a school's curriculum be devoted primarily to developing workers prepared for the demands of the global marketplace or should the development of good human beings and good citizens be an equal priority? Should school be where we attempt to address concerns about prejudice, broken homes, drug and alcohol abuse, and issues of teenage gangs?

These are issues that challenge educational leaders to confront, respectfully but vigorously, the values, ideas, and policy recommendations of leaders in other professions—politicians and corporate leaders to mention just

two—to publicly engage them in debate about what schools might reason-
ably be expected to accomplish in these areas and what kinds of support
they will need to do the job effectively.

A few years before I left my position as a principal in a public school in
the United States to assume a position as a principal at an international
school, I was challenged during a school budget presentation at a town
meeting by a well-known heckler. The heckler suggested that, given the
town's fiscal constraints, educators like me and my colleagues should demonstrate our commitment to children, if we had any, by agreeing to roll
back our salaries by 3 percent. He, too, was a town employee and there was
silence in the hall when I asked him politely but pointedly if he and his
colleagues were willing to show the way by doing what he was suggesting
others should do.

Was the silence approval or disapproval of my challenge? It was hard to
tell in that highly charged environment. The point is that it would have
been easier to let a cynical comment like his pass. But at what price? At
the price of letting a self-righteous bully characterize a group of committed
educators as selfish and indifferent to the needs of school children if they
didn't agree to roll back their already meager salaries.

There are also tests of courage that school leaders face on a daily basis
within their own schools: dysfunctional and/or disgruntled teachers, high-
maintenance parents, out-of-control kids, and communities, who, while
they say they value education, often don't value it enough to support teachers by giving them proper respect for their judgment and professionalism.

During my career as a school leader I have faced threats of physical
violence and character assassination from teachers, parents, and students.
There are few school leaders who have never had to face such threats; I
don't personally know of any. With the advent of the Internet, there is even
greater risk that a disgruntled individual can severely damage or even destroy a school leader's reputation with false accusations.

The leader's challenge is to persevere in the face of what are often very
real threats. I have come home on more than one occasion and slept on the
couch in the living room thinking that if an individual came to do what he
or she threatened to do, my wife and children had at least a fighting chance
of escaping the consequence. But even when no such threat is at hand, it is
no easy task to face the resentment of a disgruntled employee, the wrath of
an unhappy parent, or the rage of a student who is out of control and has
to be disciplined.

Every week educational leaders face tests that challenge them to exercise
the courage of their convictions. Why then don't we talk much about the
courage of educational leaders? Why don't we recognize and celebrate more
often the courage demonstrated by our leader colleagues? Does a false sense
of humility keep us from doing this or is it that we just don't consider cour-

age as worthy of notice as other leadership qualities such as vision, focus, and trust, for instance? Whatever the reason(s) we need to reassess the cost of such an omission.

Those who will one day join us in educational leadership positions need to know that courage is a quality they will need in abundance, and those of us already in leadership roles need to support one another by talking more openly about the tests of courage we've had to face.

Courage doesn't demand that we win every battle, only that we don't run away from them. We need to talk more about the courage we are called upon to display as educational leaders, we need to acknowledge the need for it in our leadership literature and leadership seminars, and we need to recognize and celebrate examples of it when we see them.

There are heroic educational leaders both today and in education's past, just as there are military heroes and sports heroes and heroes in the business world, but we seldom hear about or celebrate the heroes in our profession, and that is an oversight that must be changed. It is not hubris to recognize and celebrate courage in education; it is inspirational. Doing so inspires those who are currently in the profession and those who may one day have the courage to join it.

14

A Principal Must Protect the Social Ecology of the School

> People deal too much with the negative, with what's wrong. Why not try and see positive things, to just touch those things and make them bloom.
>
> —Tich Nhat Hanh

One of a principal's most daunting challenges these days is to protect the social ecology of his school or in some cases to work to rejuvenate an already damaged one.

Schools are social habitats whose ecology is every bit as fragile as a river's or a saltwater marsh's, and most schools' ecologies have been under duress since 1973 when the *A Nation at Risk* (1983) report declared: "The educational foundations of our society are presently being eroded by a rising tide of mediocrity that threatens our very future as a nation and a people."

Ever since that defining report, public school education in the United States has been presented to the public as if it were the Titanic after it had plowed into the iceberg. The apocalyptic descriptions of the state of American education buttressed by the punitive measures of No Child Left Behind (NCLB) have had a toxic effect on the social ecology of many schools.

One need look no further than the rise in violence in schools, the increase in dropout rates in inner-city schools, the stampede of teachers out of teaching, and the desperate efforts of communities searching for almost anyone willing to step forward to replace the teachers they are losing. The social ecology of the nation's schools is deteriorating before our very eyes and once destroyed we may have great difficulty restoring it. Thus, it falls to the school leader—the principal—to protect the social ecology of his school.

What am I talking about when I use the term *social ecology*? I'm talking about an ecosystem of relationships, the interactions of people in the school: the daily dealings of teachers with students, students with one another, and staff members with one another, with parents, and with other community members. If those relationships are damaged or destroyed, then the goals of even the most ardent school reformers are likely to suffer the fate of the Titanic. This is particularly true if the relationships between students and their teachers are poisoned by policies and press reports that are toxic to that relationship. It is the ecosystem of these very vital relationships that is now most endangered in schools. Let's take a closer look at why.

William Durden, president of Dickinson College, in prescient remarks made to international principals in 2004 warned that there are movements afoot (read NCLB) that want to turn teachers into technicians and their students into widgets. The means they use to accomplish this goal are the processes of standardization: common curriculums, standardized tests, and one-size-fits-all teaching techniques (often referred to as scientifically proven teaching approaches). Those who doubt the appeal of standardizing education and transforming teachers into technicians need look no further than the curriculum, assessments, and teaching methods of the University of Phoenix which has done both.

The problems with this approach should be obvious. To begin with, children are not widgets and no education worthy of the name should attempt to make them so. Such an approach, although we've too often taken a factory approach to education over the years, is, at best, training, and at worst, indoctrination. Whatever you choose to call it, such an "education" violates the aim that American education has had from the time of our founding fathers—to develop productive, informed, critically thoughtful citizens, many of whom will one day be leaders in their chosen field.

Another problem with the standardization approach is that effective teachers aren't the ones who are merely technicians. To be sure, effective teachers know the techniques of their craft, but their real skill lies in their ability to, if I may paraphrase Tich Nhat Hanh, touch students and make them bloom.

Technicians, no matter how skilled they may be, are not expected to inspire, affirm, and nurture those they work with. Teachers are expected to do just that. That's where this issue of the social ecology of schools comes in and becomes vitally important. If a teacher was an absolute master at the techniques of teaching reading but couldn't relate to or reach his or her students, of what use would he or she be to them?

So the first task of a principal determined to protect the social ecology of his school is to resist this standardization—not standards, not even standardized tests (which used wisely serve useful purposes) but standardization.

To resist standardization principals must themselves recognize and respect the artistry of teachers and the uniqueness of children. Then they must call attention to both publicly, and identify, verbally and in writing, as often as they can, the many ways that young people can become successful in the United States: Bill Gates and Steve Jobs never finished college, Dolly Parton never went to college, nor did Walt Disney, and architect Frank Lloyd Wright never even attended high school.

Individually and collectively, principals must point out to other Americans that a democracy cannot afford schools in which teachers operate as technicians. Nor can it allow schools that are determined to turn children into homogenized, simonized widgets. On a practical level this will require principals to speak out verbally and in writing about the aims and demands of a democratic education. They may even have to create opportunities and venues for expressing these views.

A number of other factors will make the principal's task of protecting the social ecology of a school a daunting one. The constant battering of students and their teachers in the press since 1973 has had a demoralizing effect on both. Who would want to stay aboard the Titanic if they had an opportunity to get off? Who can remain eternally motivated when stories of their futility and failure are all they hear or read about? A few of the very heroic perhaps, but not many.

The fact that politicians, corporate leaders, and the press have little sense about what it takes to motivate children and those who work with them doesn't help. If they did, it would make the principal's job easier but they don't; so the principal and other school leaders must move ahead without them and often in opposition to them.

Principals must find ways to accentuate the positive in their schools and publicize it. What education needs now more than ever is more affirmation and less defamation. Look at the Tich Nhat Hanh quote. Notice what makes things bloom. If American education is to bloom, we have to nurture it with the attitude Tich Nhat Hanh recommends, not with the coercive approach NCLB uses.

I've said that politicians, corporate people, and the press have little sense of what motivates teachers. That's because what motivates them does not motivate teachers. Unlike people in the corporate world, educators didn't enter education primarily to make money; unlike politicians, most educators aren't interested in pursuing power; and unlike members of the press, educators are far more interested in celebrating success than focusing on failure.

Those in education came into it to make a difference in the lives of children and by doing this to make a contribution to the strength of a nation. That's why they don't respond particularly well to merit pay schemes and why denigrating their effort and trying to coerce them with rewards and punishments will work against the goal of improving education.

Don't mistake me; I'm not suggesting that a principal adopt the role of a wide-eyed Pollyanna. That would be as irresponsible as the behavior of the critics I'm decrying. But the reality is that negativity has been the focus of discussions about American education for too long now, and what I said about dealing with the chronically cranky is equally true in this larger case. The principal has to counteract the negativity of past and recent apocalyptic national educational reports.

It helps that the dire predictions of these reports have proven untrue; it helps if the principal knows about research studies like the Scandia report that have unveiled the flawed analyses of these apocalyptic reports and uses them in discussions about education. But that won't be enough. As we have seen in a number of cases like the Duke Lacrosse rape scandal, the correction never gets the attention of the sensational original.

Those working in schools (children and teachers) as well as the American public need a positive foundation to build on rather than a negative swamp to sink into. Here is the terrible alternative to taking a more positive approach. If American education continues to be battered by the negativity of those who revel in it, this battering will eventually destroy the optimism that fertilizes hope in public schools and makes those working in them bloom. Instead, we will replace that hope with disillusionment, confusion, and doubt. Teachers and students will become more tense and irritable in dealing with one another as their sense of futility about what they are doing grows. Frustration and anxiety will replace optimism and the ecosystem of the school will be destroyed.

Robert Flaherty notes that there is a saying among prospectors. I don't know Robert Flaherty or where he came across this quote but it is certainly apropos to the current situation in education: "Go looking for one thing and that is all you'll ever find" (Flaherty). Since 1973 critics of American education have been looking for only one thing—its faults. And while there are faults to find, "there is gold in them thar hills as well." That's part of a principal's task in protecting the social ecology of schools: to help people to discover the gold and to mine it. It can be done.

Over time we've come to appreciate how fragile our natural environment can be and how easily we can destroy it through carelessness. It took a while but now that we have recognized the danger we've begun to take action to prevent further damage and help it to recover. To be sure there are still major threats like global warming, and much more remains to be done. But if nothing else, we are much more aware of what we must do to protect that environment than we were forty years ago when I used to drive out to the woods with my father to dump our trash.

Now we must pay attention to another ecological disaster we are creating—the one in our schools. Principals must take the lead in making sure we do pay attention.

15

When Will *We* Ever Learn?

In *Learning by Heart*, author-educator Roland Barth reveals a seldom-acknowledged truth about life in schools: "Life under the roof of the schoolhouse is toxic to adult learning" (p. 23). Certainly we all know educators in their forties, fifties, and sixties who continue to be insatiable learners, but Barth writes that the longer a teacher or principal remains in a school the less likely their learning will continue. This is an observation that my years working in schools around the world confirms.

While we pay lip service to the idea of school as a community of learners, the truth is we still maintain school communities that consist of the "learned" and the learners. There may be a number of reasons for this, including the fact that the energy needed for teaching is enormous and the many demands on teachers and school leaders are exhausting. Nonetheless, the fact that teachers and principals have aborted their learning is carcinogenic not only for their own growth but also for their students' development. Why?

One of the most potent influences that a teacher can exert on his or her students is to infect them with his or her own passion for learning. How many stories have we heard of teachers whose enthusiasm for what they were teaching ignited students' enthusiasm? In *Practicing History* Barbara Tuchman describes the effect that one professor, C. H. McLLwain, had on her.

> It did not matter to McLLwain, a renowned scholar and historian, that only four of us were taking his course, or that he had already given it at Harvard and had come over [to Radcliff] to repeat it to us (yes, that was the quaint custom of the time). It did not matter because McLLwain was conducting a passionate

affair with the laws of the Angles and the articles of the Charter, especially, as I remember, Article 39. *Like any person in love, he wanted to let everyone know how beautiful was the object of his affection.* . . . And though I cannot remember a word of Article 39, I remember how his blue eyes blazed as he discussed it and how I sat on the edge of my seat too, and how to show my appreciation, I would have given anything to write a brilliant exam paper. (p.14; italics mine)

But who can inspire another with a passion that is no longer burning in him or her? As educators we would all do well to remember that the flame of our own passion for anything is kept burning by our continued engagement with it.

In *The Artist's Way* (1992), author-artist Julia Cameron acknowledges this truth. She writes that while people much prefer to focus on having learned a skill or produced a work of art, it is infinitely more satisfying to the soul to be able to say "I'm writing a screenplay" than "I've written a screenplay" or that "I'm taking an acting class" rather than "I've taken an acting class" (p.139). This is one reason why teachers and principals must remain committed to continuing their own intellectual growth. The mantra of a teacher should be: I haven't *learned* to teach; I'm *learning* to teach. The mantra of a principal, regardless of his age, should be: I'm *learning* to lead.

As educational leader, the principal has the responsibility for ensuring that the conditions that are toxic to student learning are eliminated. The lack of opportunities for adult learning in schools is one of those toxins. How might a principal address this problem? There are the traditional staff development workshops to fall back on but I'd like to recommend three other low-cost, high-payback options.

INSIST THAT TEACHERS VISIT ONE ANOTHER'S CLASSROOMS

Rather than *encouraging* such visits I'd recommend that principals *insist* that teachers visit each other's classrooms. The benefits of such visits are simply too great to be left to chance. Any principal who has ever entered a teacher's classroom to conduct an observation knows how much can be learned about effective and ineffective classroom practices during those visits.

As a principal I learned more from my visits to teachers' classrooms than I ever did in all the methods courses and workshops I ever attended. (See "Good Teaching Ideas Observed" at the end of this chapter for examples.) Parker Palmer's observation that if doctors and lawyers lived in the same kind of self-imposed isolation as teachers we'd still treat patients with leeches and dunk defendants in mill ponds (1998, p. 144) is as damningly true today as it was when he wrote it years ago.

While it won't be easy for principals to change this deep-seated self-imposed isolation of teachers, principals have the authority and the responsibility to do so. In one school where I served as principal, I gave all department heads a day off from their classes so that they could follow a student's schedule for the entire day and view classes from the perspective of a student. Not every department head was enthusiastic in the beginning about my gift, but the results were remarkable.

We had our liveliest department heads' meeting the following day. Department heads talked about everything from how difficult it was to sit in those uncomfortable student desks for fifty minutes to how lessons that varied classroom activities without changing the focus of a lesson were the most interesting and productive ones. All of the department heads agreed that it was a day well spent and that we should give teachers an opportunity to visit classes.

Breaching the polite ironclad restriction that keeps teachers from visiting colleagues' classes is a task that educational leaders simply have to exercise the courage to tackle. A principal who reduces, if not eliminates, the conviction that teachers are in private practice will help to promote not only their growth but their students' growth as well.

FORM FACULTY STUDY GROUPS

A second strategy for encouraging adult learning in schools is to form a study group (or several of them) to research and address specific issues of teaching and learning. We are all familiar with the popularity of book discussion groups. Faculties in many schools are already part of these groups. Why not form a study group made up of selected or self-selected faculty members to study a perplexing school issue like how to increase student motivation or improve writing skills?

Japanese teachers have pioneered the practice of lesson study. Teachers in the same department come together and design a lesson. One of them then teaches the lesson while the others sit in the class and observe students' response to the lesson. The group then reconvenes and discusses what worked and what was problematic and then adjusts the lesson to make it more effective. Eventually they all teach the newly constructed lesson and further analyze its effectiveness. This has proven to be a beneficial instructional strategy that enhances not only student learning but also adult learning.

GROUP DISCUSSION ABOUT THE TEACHING LIFE

We talk a good deal in schools about students and teaching technique and very little about the demands and rewards of the teaching life itself. That is a shame and adds to the potential for exhaustion and despair. Most of what we experience and feel as educators we keep to ourselves except for occasional outbursts of frustration. That's not only shameful but harmful. What we need is a compassionate forum in which we are encouraged to express our deepest feelings about teaching. Teaching or leading a school can be a very enervating experience in which we are constantly giving and all too seldom getting enough back to re-energize ourselves.

I remember as a first-year teacher going home every afternoon and falling asleep. I worried constantly through most of that year that I might be suffering from a serious illness. One day I shared my concern with a teacher who had been in the profession for a while. I told her that prior to taking this job as a teacher I'd attended college classes, played basketball, and worked part-time three nights a week and seldom got to bed before 2 a.m. I confessed I was never as exhausted then as I was now each day after school. The veteran chuckled and told me not to worry; I probably wasn't ill but only tired from having to be "on" all day long. She was, I learned, absolutely right.

Those of us who educate others need a forum in which to acknowledge to ourselves and to one another that the demands of our profession take a lot out of us. This is one way to keep each other motivated and aflame with passion for what we do. A principal should structure time and opportunity for faculty to have discussions about the demands and challenges of the profession but also its joys and rewards as well.

None of the previously mentioned adult learning activities are particularly complicated and yet they are not simple to establish either. Most people who work in schools have simply not fully acknowledged that adult learning is vital to the vitality of the institution and the motivation of its students and have not made different methods of promoting that learning a priority.

Determined school leaders can change that by making at least one of these learning initiatives the focus of their yearly goals and by providing the time, the structure, and the imperative for faculty, including the principal, to engage in them. We can encourage students' learning by encouraging adult learning.

GOOD TEACHING IDEAS OBSERVED
IN RANDOM CLASSROOM VISITS

"Hands do the talking," the teacher I was observing said ignoring the answers several students had blurted out as if she hadn't even heard them. "John, your hand is up; what's the answer?" There were no reprimands for offenders; only positive reinforcement for those who met her expectations. Three weeks later when I observed the same class I immediately noticed that whenever the teacher asked a question hands shot up and no one shouted out an answer.

"Stand up," the teacher said. "Today we are going to learn division and addition of fractions; so I want you all to go out into the corridor and form a straight line." That accomplished, she asked them to *divide* their line in half, then quarters, then eighths, and sixteenths. Then she had them *recombine* into eighths, quarters, half, and whole again. And so began a bodily kinesthetic introduction into adding and dividing fractions.

The students certainly didn't expect to find a stone wall constructed of cardboard and brick construction paper separating them from their teacher when they entered their English class for a discussion of Robert Frost's "Mending Wall." But that is exactly what they got. And by lesson's end they understood what Frost meant by "something there is that doesn't love a wall" and "before I built a wall I ask to know what I was walling in or walling out."

16

Discipline Isn't a Dirty Word

By the time the bus carrying the students and their chaperones returning from a three-day field trip pulled into the school driveway I knew I'd be dealing with half a dozen students who had been discovered drinking in their hotel rooms. I'd spoken by phone with the head chaperone and knew the details of the incident. I'd had some time to reflect on the kind of disciplinary action we might take.

When the students disembarked, the head chaperone led the offenders to my office. He and I had discussed what would come next; so, he was not surprised when I told the students that no decision had been made on the disciplinary action we would take. That decision would be made after I had met with all the trip chaperones that afternoon and after I had met with each student and his or her parents the following morning.

I sent the students home with a letter from me asking that each parent meet with me the following morning. I told the students that it was their responsibility to tell their parents why this meeting was necessary. After cautioning them about why they should not downplay the seriousness of the incident, or their part in it, when they told their parents, I sent them on their way. My own experience as a child had taught me that the anticipation of an unknown consequence often prompted more remorse than the consequence itself.

The chaperones and I then met. We'd already had some discussion by phone about possible consequences; the easiest to administer would be a three-day out-of-school suspension, but we had some concerns about this.

To begin with, many of the students' parents were working during the day and had no way of supervising their kids during a three-day suspension. But there was another compelling factor that made a three-day out-of-school suspension less appealing as a consequence. We were a school with five core values that drove the decisions we made on virtually everything. The students had violated at least two of those core values, sense of self and respect for all, and we wanted them to understand that and to appreciate the impact of that violation on the school community.

So, in the end, we agreed on a different disciplinary route. The students would be suspended for a day in school and during that suspension they would have to do research on a number of questions we designed related to their infraction. (See "Questions Field Trip Students Were Expected to Address" at the end of the chapter.) The research would include interviews as well as library and Internet work.

But that wasn't all. The students would also be required to present the results of their research at the end of the school day to a panel of their parents, the trip chaperones, and me. The students would be expected to present as a group and each member of the group would have to play an equal role. The quality of the research and the presentation would be assessed by the adult panel using a rubric we designed for that purpose.

When I met with the parents the following day there was some resistance, but not much. The biggest obstacle to overcome was that many of the parents worked and would have to leave work early to participate on the panel as we required. But, as I've said, the school has a very strong set of core values and parents understand their significance in our school community life; in the end every parent accepted the disciplinary action.

As for the students and their presentation: while some students' presentation skills were less than we might have hoped for (no doubt due to their anxiety over the panel they were presenting to), the quality of their research, and their collective and individual ability to answer questions about what they had learned from their mistake, was superb. It was obvious they had internalized the lesson we wanted then to learn; every adult left the meeting confident of that.

When you ask an adolescent "What is discipline?" invariably you get the same reply. "Punishment." Not infrequently, you get a similar response from adults. This may explain why so few youngsters welcome discipline and why so many adults feel uncomfortable when they have to discipline children. "If discipline is punishment, who needs it?"

But discipline has really gotten a bad rap. While punishment is one of its many definitions, it is by no means the primary one. In fact, in *Webster's New World Dictionary of the American Language* (1968), it is the last one, reluctantly squeezed in there, it seems, with all those other definitions that have to do with teaching, training, and the development of personal control. The word *discipline* actually comes from the Latin root word meaning *to learn*. It's a close relative of the word *disciple*, meaning *pupil*.

What then is discipline and how can a principal and teachers utilize it so that it becomes a constructive part of our children's growth and development? The dictionary supplies a healthy, affirmative definition: "training that develops self-control, character or orderliness and efficiency." Discipline should be part of the training we give children in order that they may gain self-control and develop the character they need to master and control their own lives. It is a gift of love, not a form of retribution. Acknowledging this we approach the task of disciplining children with firmness, fairness, consistency, and patience, fully expecting that all children can learn what we want them to learn.

The function of our discipline is not to give adults ultimate control over youngsters' lives, but rather to give it to them. Caring adults, parents, teachers, coaches, and others fulfill their roles in youngsters' lives by providing the support, guidance, and training necessary to help the young develop the conduct they must have to become truly independent. They help children to develop an understanding of the need for a proper balance between their own needs and desires and the needs and desires of others.

As children grow up these same adults willingly surrender more and more of the control over youngsters' lives to them, allowing them to make more decisions for themselves and expecting them to accept responsibility for those decisions

Effective disciplinarians always take the time to reflect on what they want their discipline to teach and structure it so that the lesson is clear. Disciplining without a clear objective in mind is like trying to teach algebra or Shakespeare without a lesson plan: little learning will take place, and when it does, it will often be the wrong kind. I know a boy whose mother attempted to solve the problem of his cussing by feeding him a tablespoon of hot mustard every time she heard him utter a purple expression. He's a man now and still cussing, but he won't go near mustard.

PRINCIPLES OF GOOD DISCIPLINE

- Discipline without anger (even if you have to wait a while until your anger is under control). Refer to the disciplinary actions you take as "consequences" rather than "punishment."
- Help the disciplined youngster process what happened and why, and then work with him or her to develop a plan to address the problem so it doesn't re-occur.
- Avoid inconsistency—addressing a behavior one time and allowing it to pass at another time because you are too busy.
- Resist the urge not to discipline because you feel sorry for a youngster. You can empathize with how a youngster is feeling about the mistake

that he or she made but letting him or her escape the consequences of his or her action is a mistake you don't want to make.

- Separate the deed from the doer in your own mind and in the mind of the offender. It is not uncommon for a student you are disciplining to feel that, because of what he or she has done, you don't like him or her. Make it clear that it is the action you cannot accept, not him or her.
- Make the point with a youngster clearly and concisely. If you go on and on, a youngster will learn to tune you out. Deaf ears do not respond well to correction.
- Catch a youngster whose been disciplined being good (regularly) and acknowledge it. A carrot is a better motivator than the stick, and healthier, too.

The demands to discipline are tough on both the discipliner and the disciplined. That is why discipline is considered by some as a dirty word. But the rewards of discipline are great, the penalties for lack of it extreme, especially in adulthood. We admire the discipline of our athletes, our artists, our scientists, and our scholars. We would not think of sending an undisciplined army onto the field of battle. Discipline isn't a dirty word. If we discipline children properly, they will in time come to understand that—and, who knows, they may even someday be grateful to us for it.

QUESTIONS FIELD TRIP STUDENTS WERE EXPECTED TO ADDRESS

- Which of the school's core values have you violated by your actions and in what ways have you violated them? (Be specific in your answer. A general statement that you shouldn't be drinking will not be acceptable.)
- In what ways have you disappointed your parents, your chaperones, your fellow trip members, the school community, and yourself?
- What does research say about teenage drinking and alcoholism?
- If you were again confronted with the opportunity to drink on another trip, what *specific strategies* would you use to keep yourself and your fellow students from doing it?
- What is the most important lesson that you personally have learned from this experience?

17

"Seek the Story Within": Interview to Reveal the Heart of a Teacher

"Seek the story within." This advice was meant for aspiring writers. But it serves those who interview teaching candidates equally as well. Every teacher has a story—or should. The story reveals the secrets of a teacher's passion for learning and teaching—if there is any. But too often interviews are conducted like autopsies. They are cold, clinical evaluations of the candidate's experience and expertise, but they fail to feel for a pulse.

This is not meant to denigrate the examination of a candidate's teaching background and teaching proficiency; an interviewer should probe both. But, if that is all the interview uncovers, a principal has failed to do his job.

Teaching success hinges upon more than just experience and craft knowledge. Effective teachers are aflame with a passion for children and ablaze with a love of teaching. If they are not, can we expect them to ignite a love of learning in children? An interviewer who fails to unearth a teacher's passion, assuming it's there, is like a geologist who studies the surface of a volcano and ignores the burning magma beneath. Seek the story within. The story tells us not just what the teacher knows and has done, it bares his or her soul.

What do you get when you unearth the story? One candidate for a science position told me about spending the year past as a volunteer researcher observing osprey in their habitat. The excitement in his voice as he described sitting alone on an island in Maine recording his observations as the seasons changed from humid to cool, to cold, to rainy, and back again told me he could inspire in students a love of science and an appreciation for scientists who make great sacrifices to observe, record, analyze, and help us understand our natural world better. There was magic in the story and excitement in the voice that related it.

Seek the story within sounds easy and reasonable enough, but, like most things that appear easy in the hands of a skillful practitioner, getting the story within out isn't easy. To do it, an interviewer must overcome certain urges, must deliberately craft thought-provoking questions, and must get each candidate comfortable enough to tell his or her story. Let's start with the urges.

Interviewers can be like Trappist monks who've been given a reprieve from their vow of silence. The interviewer does the talking while the candidate listens respectfully. The principal wants to be likeable and engaging, wants to sell himself and his school to the candidate. That's fine, but when a principal is talking, the candidate isn't, and precious minutes during which his or her story could be told are being lost. So while we don't want an interview to be conducted like an inquisition, an interviewer needs to provide the interviewee opportunity to reveal his or her story. There will be time later to sell the school and himself, in a call-back interview, for instance.

"Interviewing," writes John Brady in *Popping the Questions*, "is the modest immediate science of gaining trust and then gaining information" (p. 69). An interviewer needs to know what he is after and how to go after it. He must prepare for an interview before meeting the candidate by reading his dossier and highlighting important points to pursue with him. The interviewer then crafts a set of questions he plans to ask, not counting on being able to formulate the best questions under what Brady calls "battlefield conditions."

The questions should be thought-provoking questions that compel a candidate to speak freely. Getting to the story within requires an avaricious elegance of inquiry that refuses to be satisfied with surface answers. Like Ahab pursuing his whale, an interviewer must be intent on probing the "lower layers." Watch a skilled interviewer at work: Barbara Walters, Bill Moyers, Larry King, and Mike Wallace. They are bottom feeders, never satisfied with lip surface answers. They know the compelling stories lie in an interviewee's heart and stomach.

Once the questions have been formulated, the skillful interviewer weaves them into a pattern that puts the candidate at ease and makes it easier for him to tell his story. But the interviewer must not cling so tightly to questions that he misses opportunities to hear interesting side trips by insisting candidates always stick to the main road. If a candidate veers off onto an interesting side road, go with him; who knows what may be hidden there.

Sometimes the Scheherezade stories are found down a side road while the main drag turns out to be "a real drag." People plan sequentially but they don't talk that way—unless they're real bores. If a candidate strays too far away from a question to no purpose, a skillful interviewer brings him back with a refocusing question.

A good way to prepare for interviewing is to watch videos of skillful interviewers doing them. Libraries usually have audio and video tapes featuring Bill Moyers, Edward R. Murrow, Mike Wallace, and others interviewing famous people. As you watch you'll see how a successful interviewer puts his subject at ease by beginning with easy, rather routine questions and then moves to the more robust and challenging ones. Note how the interviewer knows when to listen, when to probe, and when to let go of an idea. Learn from the experts.

Brady offers several other helpful tips. Avoid the filibuster question—the one that takes longer for the interviewer to ask than the candidate to answer. As a general rule, he says, the longer the question, the shorter the reply (p. 76). Avoid leading questions—ones that suggest the answer in your tone, inflection, or phrasing (p. 77). "You wouldn't take a job you weren't completely comfortable with, would you?" If you have to explore an area like that, it would be better to ask: "Have you ever taken a job or assignment you weren't completely comfortable with?" Or "Under what conditions would you take a job or an assignment you weren't completely comfortable with?"

Avoid the cliché question—the one the candidate is likely to be asked in every interview. For instance, "What would you do if you disagreed with an administrative decision?" If the candidate hasn't prepared half a dozen sanctimonious banalities in answer to that question, you are probably his or her first interview. Think of a better way to ask a question like that that will make a candidate be specific in his or her answer. "Could you give me an example of a time when . . . ?" And remember to listen rather than feed when you're seeking the story within. Silence often encourages rather than discourages a revealing response.

And finally, what is the abracadabra word for getting the genie out of the bottle when you want a candidate to tell his or her story? It is the simple word *when*, says Brady (p. 74). "When did you realize you'd made a mistake?" or "When did you first realize you wanted to be a teacher?" The word *when* takes a person back to a scene, a setting, and thence to the story. The devil may lie in the details, but the heart of the teacher lies in the story. Seek the story within.

18

What a Revolting Development This Is!: The Homework Rebellion

Parents are revolting! No, this isn't the summary judgment of a teenager about parents. It's true; there really is a revolution out there among parents, a revolt against, can you believe this, homework.

In increasing numbers, parents are expressing dissatisfaction about children coming home with homework. In one American city, the mayor took things into his own hands mandating that children be assigned no more than an hour and a half of homework per evening. His proclamation was greeted with widespread enthusiasm among adult constituents, and one can easily imagine the mayor has guaranteed himself a significant voter base among the young for generations to come.

The mutiny over homework has two major causes. Homework, say some, is compromising family life by shortening the time families share in the evening. The busy workday lives of parents and school children leave little time for "family" during the day. Both parents in many families, when a family is fortunate enough to have two parents, are often working. In addition, the length of the school day and number of days in school have been extended for many students in many countries. When you add the fact that many students have active lives in athletics and other school activities once classes are over, that leaves less time for family togetherness.

A second cause for homework unhappiness is the conflict that often occurs when parents have to battle with children to "get that homework done." The result of all of this is that homework, which was formerly viewed by parents as a beneficial addition to school and family life (at least that is how parents viewed it when I was a student), is now being increasingly seen as a parasite on family life.

I am not unsympathetic with the argument that too much homework can create problems for parents and their children. Frankly, I find a renewed interest in family togetherness refreshing, especially if togetherness means more than merely being together for isolated, individual pursuits. And, an average of one and a half hours of homework a night should be quite sufficient if we educators are genuinely committed to helping children develop a well-balanced life. Indeed, homework in proper proportion can be part of developing that balance.

"Impossible," you say.

Consider this: In an age as fast-paced and frenetic as ours, many of our families' days whirl away in a bedlam of activity leaving little time for repose and reflection. The slogan "Just Do It" implies we don't have time to appreciate the value of anything we're doing; we merely have time to do it.

Many children today are consciously and subconsciously internalizing this message and are living thoughtlessly. Their lives are packed with activity. They remind one of little Sammy Glick in Budd Shulberg's *What Makes Sammy Run.* Their parents, running around trying to keep up with them, have that tired and beaten look of a Willy Lowman. What is missing from many families' lives and what homework time can provide is "quiet time" for the entire family—time for reflection and recapitulation.

It takes discipline to slow down and reflect on what one is doing—and learning. This discipline must be taught, learned, and practiced until it becomes a habit. Youngsters do not inherit it as a birthright, nor does it come naturally as a product of their development from childhood to adulthood. Indeed, young people (and adults who have never learned the value of reflection) are much more naturally inclined to the "Just Do It" than to think about what they are doing, how they are doing it, and why they are doing it.

"Homework time," properly balanced with other valued evening family pursuits, can provide opportunity for the entire family to rest and reflect. It can help youngsters develop a discipline that will serve them well for a lifetime. Homework need not be a source of anarchy in the household. The answer to frustration with it does not lie in abandoning it altogether as clutter in a busy family's life that compromises its togetherness.

No, homework has genuine value, and children and the adults who care about them should renew their covenant with it rather than condemning it. In our own home, when our four children were in school, my wife and I established a routine of one and a half hours of quiet time for study and reading each evening. Over the course of time we and our children looked forward to that time.

Principals' and teachers' part of that covenant is to ensure that time spent on homework is reasonable and worthwhile. That means teachers' homework assignments should be challenging, interesting (rather than merely drill and practice), and able to be completed in time to give their students opportunity to enjoy some evening free time. It means also that a principal needs to have in place a structure in which he can monitor how much homework is being assigned by teachers to their classes each night. Parents' part is to make homework time valued in the home. Students' part is to approach homework as worthy of their best effort.

When this is done, homework will prove to be rewarding rather than revolting—for all. (See appendix 2 for guidelines that you can put on handouts to help parents monitor their children's homework without creating major family conflict.)

19

How Do You Spell Friendship?: The Intergenerational Spelling Bee

"An Irish teacher is trying to assist her struggling fourth graders recall the meaning of the word *cannibal*," I declare in my best imitation Irish brogue. "In an effort to prod their faulty memories, she says to one of them: 'Shamus, we studied this yesterday in social studies. If you were to eat your mother and father, what would they be calling you now?'"

Pausing before the punch line, I glance out at the perplexed faces of my senior citizen audience. They are wondering what I, a middle school principal, am doing here in their meeting hall. *Have I come to ask them for money or to support the school budget in the upcoming town meeting?*

"Finally, after turning the question over in his mind a couple of times," I continue, tugging at my tie à la Rodney Dangerfield, "Shamus ventures with anything but assurance: 'an orphan?'"

Laughter fills the hall and everyone relaxes a bit; still they wonder: *Why has he come here?* Theirs is not a territory into which many educators venture. So, after a few more jokes that played well at my own dinner table, I tell them. "We, my sixth grade companions and I, are here to recruit some of you for a Sixth Grade/Senior Citizens Spelling Bee we are planning." A slight but audible gasp stirs through the hall.

The spelling bee is the brainchild of John McSheehy, one of the teachers who has accompanied me here. He takes the microphone to explain the concept and tell why we need senior citizens to make it work.

It's simple really. Youngsters spend five and a half hours each day in school learning skills we say they will use someday as members of society. But do they believe us? Or do they think that this is little more than "teacher talk"? At Varnum Brook Middle School we want them to learn that the skills they are mastering now are valued and used by members of society. Seated in front of us in this senior citizens hall are the adults who can help us convey this message. Will they accept the challenge?

We know that senior citizens, many of whom have little contact with youngsters, are often fearful of them. In newspapers they read about acts of violence committed by children and see examples of it on TV. We want them to know the middle school students we see every day: affectionate, idealistic, not unflawed, but nonetheless hard-working students who are solicitous about others and involved in their community. We would like seniors to see that middle school youngsters today have much in common with the children they were forty or fifty years ago.

If we could accomplish that, a special bond of friendship could be forged between one generation and another. Our students would benefit from such a relationship with adults who could teach them to be unafraid of accepting academic challenges. Seniors would learn to appreciate our students as community members to be valued rather than strangers to be feared.

We didn't expect that getting seniors to participate would be easy, and it wasn't. Adults often exhibit the same reluctance to risk-taking that students display. The seniors were unsure of themselves. Some worried about infirmities impairing their ability to perform; others did not want to disappoint themselves and us with a poor showing. To help allay fears, we promised to give them copies of the spelling list we would use in the competition so that they could study. We also offered them practice sessions and instituted some rules to accommodate for individual handicaps.

For instance, seniors (who might have difficulty hearing) could request to have a word repeated as many times as they liked and to hear it used in two different sentences instead of one. Those who had difficulty getting up and coming to the podium could spell a word from their seats. Above all, we stressed that winning the competition was not the important thing; teaching children the value of good spelling was. An exhibition of how one generation after another learns to practice an important academic skill was our focus. The participants would be part of a historic event, the very first Varnum Brook Sixth Grade/Senior Citizens Spelling Bee.

Convincing seniors to take the plunge required persistence, but persistence paid off. We were invited to dinner and by the time dinner was over we had recruited eight adult contestants. In the intervening six weeks before the event, we would lose two, but with half a dozen seniors remaining, we had enough to ensure that the spelling bee would be a reality.

On the day of the spelling bee, our program began with a brunch for all participants: contestants, judges, timers, and moderator. The middle school jazz band entertained us as we ate. Sixth graders introduced themselves to the seniors and the groups were given plenty of opportunity to get to know one another before the competition began.

The competition proved to be a spirited one indeed. Both sixth graders and seniors performed well. Although there was both a sixth grader and senior citizen winner, the final contestant left standing was a senior citizen—a retired English teacher who had taught for twenty-five years and had loved spelling bees as a youngster. She later revealed that she had won many of them in her early years and was delighted with the opportunity to compete in another.

When the spelling bee was over, I presented each sixth grader and senior with a certificate of participation, a school pride pin, and a letter of appreciation signed by the principal. After that, the sixth grade participants took the seniors on a tour of the school and invited them into their classes. What did the seniors think of all of this?

"This was a wonderful experience. I'm so glad I came," said one.

"These children are so lovely. You have a wonderful school," said another.

"Can we count on you to come back and join us again next year?" I asked as they prepared to leave.

"Oh yes," came the enthusiastic replies, "and we'll bring some friends with us."

Three years later when I left to take a position at an international school, the Sixth Grade/Senior Citizens Spelling Bee was still going strong. With each succeeding year it had grown in stature. Each year sixth graders and seniors looked forward to it with increased anticipation. So did the public. After the first year, it was covered by both local newspapers and had the support of an enthusiastic audience of senior citizens and sixth grade parents.

We had no difficulty finding seniors to participate after that first year. They knew that they were welcomed and appreciated by our students and staff who looked forward to their arrival. The prizes we offered—a $25 gift certificate for dinner for two at a local restaurant for the winning senior and a $50 savings bond for the winning sixth grader—are not what drew those who competed. The opportunity to meet and learn from one another is.

A society whose children are not connected with adults of previous generations, learning from them and emulating them, is a society whose children are being hurt. Grown-ups are meant to be children's guides, and youngsters expect to be taught by them, coached by them, and mentored by them. Most of all, youngsters need adults who are models of what is good and right and positive in life. Adults, too, benefit from working with young people.

In teaching children what they have been taught and assisting them in cultivating habits of the mind and heart that are necessary for successful living, grown-ups fulfill a responsibility to posterity and to our nation. In the process, they ensure a better future for themselves.

Retirees and senior citizens have fewer opportunities to influence society now than when they were younger. They welcome a chance to demonstrate that they still have something to offer. By providing occasion for members of two generations to meet on a level playing field of academic competition, the Sixth Grade/Senior Citizen Spelling Bee furthered the cause of education and built a much-needed bridge over which students and senior citizens could cross to touch each other's lives.

20

Educators' Responsibility for Creating a Public

Social critic and educator Neil Postman has written that education does not serve a public. It creates one. The question is not does or doesn't schooling create a public, he says; the question is: what kind of public does it create (1996, p. 18)?

Faced with this reality, those of us in education need to do some serious thinking about what kind of public we have a moral obligation to create and how we should go about creating it. At present, educators, in public schools at least, have little say about what kind of citizens those schools will create. The decision has been co-opted by politicians and corporate leaders. But that reality may be changing for reasons I'll discuss later in this chapter.

Most educators would, I think, agree that we do have an obligation to society in this matter of creating a public that includes but goes beyond merely carrying out the narrow utilitarian initiatives of politicians and corporate leaders that focus exclusively on producing future employees with marketable skills.

While no educational leader would argue that education shouldn't have as one of its goals to teach students the knowledge and skills that they will need to be productively employed in the marketplace, few would accept that as the only purpose of an education. James Moffett in *The Universal Schoolhouse* (1994) in words that resonate with Postman's says that "education should . . . fashion a special culture that will correct and complement society" (p. 57).

WHAT'S MISSING?

What's missing in the current educational agenda is a sense of the higher purpose of learning, the recognition that education shouldn't just train students to make a living but should teach them how to lead meaningful lives. British economist E. F. Schumacher recognized this. He said that the task of education should be, first and foremost, "the transmission of ideas of value of what to do with our lives." He called an education that focuses primarily on producing "know how" "a mere potentiality, and unfinished sentence" (1973, pp. 74–75).

The hollowness of our current approach of focusing education on preparing students for the job market is not lost on students. It leaves them with a sense of "Is that all there is?" It is the reason so many of them drop out of school before finishing and why so many others sit passively in classes struggling to endure education rather than learning to love it.

Young people, like the rest of us, are looking for ideas that give meaning to their lives. They recognize that man is meant to work to live, but not live to work. The words of those who trumpet the virtues of 24/7 sound discordant to them. They want an education that helps them sort through their various longings, desires, and urges. They want an education that helps them answer the questions: Why am I here? What is the purpose of my life? What is beauty? What are love, happiness, honor, and virtue?

WHAT KIND OF PUBLIC DO WE NEED?

This is a compelling question that calls for thoughtful discussion in school communities. Many of these discussions may have taken place in different schools and the answers are described in the schools' mission statements and core values. Invariably mission statements speak about preparing students for purposeful lives as informed and contributing citizens. So let's start there.

John Donne reminded us four centuries ago that no man is an island. Yet too often in pursuit of personal happiness people act as though they are separate islands and that the problems of our fellow men are not our problems. A quality education should not only prepare students to have a sense of themselves and who they are in the world but should teach them to look beyond themselves to the needs of the community (i.e., local, national, and global). We seem to be losing our sense of community at a time when the world is shrinking and when what happens in one place, no matter how far away, is bound to affect us all. A good part of the answer to the questions "Why am I here?" and "What is the purpose of my life?" may be found in the following Sufi story.

> Past the seeker as he prayed came the hungry and the lame, the downtrodden, distressed and depressed. And dropping deeper into prayer the seeker cried out: "Oh dear God, how can you look upon such misery and not do something?" And down in the depths of his soul the seeker heard a voice that said: "I did do something—I made you."

This story helps us to understand the kind of public we need to create. It does not suggest that we need a public made up of only doctors, psychiatrists, social workers, and non-governmental organizations, but that we have a public that respects each individual as a person of dignity and worth. It is a public in which individuals are capable of looking beyond their personal needs to the needs of the greater community when that becomes necessary. Moreover, it is a story whose message appeals to the deepest aspirations of young people.

The kind of public we need is a public that seeks to achieve balance in life. Work is balanced with rest; the demands of the workplace are balanced with the demands of family, friends, and community; and the needs of the individual and community are correctly identified and balanced with the needs of future communities.

Decades ago C. S. Lewis pointed out that men used to create products because other men needed them. Now we create products and carry on expensive advertising campaigns to convince men they do need them. With our planet groaning under the strain of our intemperance and in danger of imploding we need a public that will take to heart Gandhi's comment that "Earth has enough to satisfy man's need, but not man's greed" (Schumacher, p. 31).

The kind of public we require will need to know how to keep other things in balance as well. Competition will have to be balanced with cooperation and collaboration, science with the humanities, academics with the arts, and "know how" with the study of metaphysics. Knowing how to do something without being able to determine why we are doing it or whether or not we should be doing it at all is a prescription for disaster. Finally, although some are reluctant to recognize this, the public we need will have to learn to balance physical and social development with moral and spiritual growth and development.

"The philosophy in the classroom of this generation," said Abraham Lincoln, "is the philosophy of the government in the next" (Zhao, p. 11). Neil Postman takes Lincoln's observation a step further. He says that the philosophy of the classroom of this generation will determine the philosophy of the public in the next. If we want good government, wise leadership, and a kind and caring community, then educators and educational leaders must create it by attending to the kind of public we are creating in our classrooms today. Recognize it or not, accept it or not, education doesn't just serve a public; it creates one.

DO WE HAVE THE COURAGE TO CREATE
THE PUBLIC THE COUNTRY NEEDS?

Roland Barth in *Learning by Heart* says that what most of those outside of schools want is educators who are bright sheep—followers (not leaders)—

educators willing to carry out *their* agendas. He goes on to point out the obvious: there is no such thing as bright sheep. Schools can have educators and educational leaders who are either bright, willful (read determined) goats or dumb, obedient plodding sheep (p. 5).

As we confront the reality that education doesn't simply serve a public but creates one, every educational leader in a school, whether he is in a classroom or the principal's office, must come to terms with his obligation to help decide what kind of public the school will create. Beyond that, individually and collectively, leaders in education will have to have the courage to fight for the education students deserve and that the country needs.

A public waits to be created. Opinion polls show that the confidence of the American people in political and corporate leaders is at an all-time low. A recent study done by the Institute for Alternative Futures for the National Association of Elementary School Principals' *Vision 20/21* predicts that the public will turn to other sectors "to find leaders to trust and respect." The stakes are high, the future waits. Are we ready to assume the leadership in creating the kind of public our country and the world needs?

21

Should Schools Offer Parent Training?

The longer I worked in education the more convinced I became that the job of an educator includes much more than just teaching the children who come into our schools each day. It involves reaching out and educating the parents of these children as well. The task of raising children to become mature, self-reliant, responsible human beings has never been an easy one; it is even more difficult these days. As educators who deal daily with children passing through the turbulent developmental years, we know the challenges that parents face. Raising children today is a constant cycle of demands and decisions. Knowing what *not* to do is just as important as knowing what to do.

Think for a minute of the countless decisions parents must make every day. Just the ones involving what children do in school seem to demand the wisdom of Aristotle, the patience of Job, and Promethean endurance. What's to be done when a child isn't doing well in school? Who is to blame? How many times have we heard a parent remark with exasperation during a discipline conference, "But what good is a suspension? I'm working and it's just a holiday for him." How should a parent respond to a suspension?

When a youngster constantly forgets his or her lunch money, books, or homework, who owns the problem: the youngster, the parent, or the teacher? What should be done about it? By the time a parent starts to feel he or she has a handle on these kinds of problems, along come the challenges of peer relationships and peer pressure. As children grow older, concerns about them experimenting with sex and drugs and alcohol become issues. Parents can hardly be blamed if they throw up their hands and exclaim in consternation, "Why don't children come with operator's manuals?"

Do parents always know what is in the best interest of their children? Do they approach the question of what is best rationally and pragmatically, or are they often making decisions primarily on instincts, hunches, and impulses generated by the emotions of the moment? Even worse, are parents practicing the same unexamined parenting techniques they learned from their own parents?

I'm not being super-critical here. As parents who have raised four children of our own, my wife and I many times found ourselves empathizing with the plaintive cry of parents who wish their children had come with an operator's manual. On more than one occasion I've found myself, at times, seriously considering taking Mark Twain's tongue-in-cheek advice on raising an adolescent: "When a child turns thirteen put him in a barrel and feed him through a small hole; and when he turns eighteen, plug up the hole" (White). Parenting is no easy matter; even experts fail us when we need them most. "When my kids become wild and unruly, I use a nice safe playpen. When they're finished, I climb out," a weary Erma Bombeck wrote (Bombeck).

Still, as educators, we enjoy a great advantage when it comes to raising and training children. We should be able to give parents more practical advice than either Twain or Bombeck. We have access to the best information available from educational research and psychology on the developmental needs of children, early adolescents, adolescents, and young adults. That knowledge is field tested 180 days or more every year, year after year. In the important area of training children, educators have much to offer parents.

But are we taking advantage of that opportunity? Shouldn't every elementary, middle, and high school offer some kind of parent effectiveness training program? I think so. It would be a humane and sensible thing to do.

Some might argue that with the time and resources available to them, teachers and principals have enough of a challenge trying to educate the children of the United States without taking on responsibility for educating their parents as well. However, since we tell parents that education is a three-way alliance of educators, students, and parents, we need to find effective ways to support parents in the difficult role they must carry out to ensure the alliance is successful. One idea worth pursuing is to offer parents the kind of child development information and training that is available to us. The best way to do this may well be parent effectiveness training workshops offered by school personnel.

WHAT KINDS OF PROGRAMS CAN SCHOOLS OFFER PARENTS?

I first became aware of parent training programs through my wife, a school counselor who has worked with several training models. In one model, parents spend a weekend away from home in a hotel where they take a variety of workshops offered by school counselors and invited guest presenters. The workshops encompass a variety of topics: reflective listening, parenting styles, "I" messages, principles for conducting an effective family meeting, the role of birth order in a family, and issues of drinking, drugs, and sexuality among adolescents.

Time spent at these retreats provides parents with relaxation away from the daily demands of their children and affords presenters and parents a concentrated uninterrupted opportunity to fully explore the subject matter of effective parenting. The experience is analogous to the one we as principals and our teachers have when attending a three-day workshop. During these weekends parents form networks and support groups. They go home feeling that they are not alone in whatever problems they may be experiencing with their youngster(s). Someone out there is contending with the same kind of problem.

Most importantly, parents return home refreshed and equipped with new information and strategies for addressing the raising of their children. Not coincidentally, they see the school in a different light, as an ally with them in promoting what's best for their children, rather than an adversary blaming them for their children's shortcomings.

Once a new spirit of working together has been established, parents are less hesitant to call the school asking for advice. They feel freer to share information about their children with those school personnel who need to know. If my wife's experience is a good barometer, they also write startlingly positive letters to the school and the newspapers about the worthwhile experiences they have had with the parenting workshops. The money to provide parents with a workshop weekend may come from grant writing or from the school budget itself.

Not all parents can manage to spend a weekend away from home, however, and not all schools can secure the grant money to offer parents the opportunity to do so. Fortunately, there are other kinds of workshop formats. One that I have used successfully follows a format similar to a university course. Parents are invited to join a parenting group by a guidance counselor. They agree to make a commitment of one night a week for six weeks.

I found that parents looked forward to these weekly sessions and came to them equipped with notebooks and materials the same way a student attending a class might. Indeed, they often told me and the counselor they enjoyed "coming to class" each week. Although the concentrated intensity of an evening is not equal to the relaxed atmosphere of a weekend retreat, parents often found the additional time to think about what they had learned in the previous week's session valuable. They had an opportunity to experiment with the techniques they had learned and then talk about them in a subsequent session. When we utilized this model I found we received exceptionally positive responses on our feedback surveys.

Finally, there is the specific topic workshop. In this format parents can select from a series of one-day workshops on a specific topic such as positive communication, parenting styles, adolescent development, or dealing with discipline. Parents select one or more of these workshops based on their needs. The school schedules sessions for Saturdays or evenings that are convenient for parents.

An effective parenting program is not difficult to organize. A school principal, counselor, drug counselor, nurse, home economics teacher, working alone or in combination, can put together a worthwhile program within a period of weeks. A number of organizations offer very good program materials and even training with these materials at a reasonable cost. Professionals from other fields (e.g., health care, legal services, law enforcement) will often donate their services as guest speakers.

Most importantly parents find the information that these workshops provide and the techniques they teach very effective. They report increased success and fulfillment as parents. There is increased satisfaction with the child's school. Everybody benefits. As such programs become established in schools, more parents hear about them and enroll in them. A special bond is forged between parents and the schools their children attend.

Effective parenting programs establish the kind of relationship that makes a true partnership between school and parents possible. These programs send an unmistakable message that adults working in schools (many of them parents themselves) recognize the complexity and demanding nature of parents' responsibility and want to help them get the information and skills they need to carry out that responsibility. That's what a partnership is all about. Finally, parenting workshops bring parents and educators together in a common cause for the healthy development and welfare of children. Good things can't help but come from that.

RESOURCES FOR PARENT EFFECTIVENESS TRAINING

Parent Effectiveness Training
Dr. Thomas Gordon

Systematic Training for Effective Parenting
American Guidance Service

Active Parenting Publishers

22

Musings

TEACHER EVALUATION

I remember saying to a colleague that teacher evaluation was a task like cleaning a chicken coop. It had to be done, but neither the cleaner nor the chickens liked it very much and the long-term results were at best dubious.

Teacher evaluation is one of the most time-consuming and least fulfilling parts of a principal's job. Add to that the research that shows that it does little to improve instruction and you have to wonder why we spend so much time on it. There is, of course, the reality that it must be done to root out those teachers who should be in another profession. But my God, the time it takes.

One of the best ways I've found to improve instruction is to encourage teachers to visit one another's classrooms not for the purpose of evaluation but to observe and learn and share professional knowledge. Aside from the fact that the visited teacher always wants to be at his or her best when there's another adult in the room, it can be an intellectually stimulating experience for both parties. The challenge is to break through the mindset that many teachers have that "I'm in private practice when I enter my classroom so visitors are an unwelcome distraction."

I found that the best evaluation conferences I've had with teachers are conferences in which I let the teacher do most of the talking. I've used this procedure for goal setting and goal assessment conferences and for classroom observation conferences. My primary role in these conferences has been to prepare and to ask good reflection questions. It's remarkable how insightful and honest most (not all) teachers can be when they have to do the talking. Getting teachers to reflect on their practice is a key to having them improve their practice.

MAKING A QUIET STATEMENT AT MEETINGS

A couple of superintendents I've worked for took note of the fact that I seldom, if ever, was the first to speak at an administration meeting (unless I was presenting a proposal), and sometimes they didn't hear from me at all on an agenda item. When I explained the reason for this they were impressed and appreciative.

I'm not by nature taciturn but I have trained myself to listen first at meetings and not to feel compelled to repeat what someone else has said unless it is necessary to emphasize my agreement with a point he or she has made. And when a decision seems to be headed in the direction I think it should, there is no reason to jump in and slow the process down. Learning to control your tongue at meetings accomplishes two things: it respects people's time (including your own) and when you do speak people are more inclined to listen attentively.

SOMETIMES YOU HAVE TO SHOW
YOU CAN'T BE INTIMIDATED

One night after I had presented my middle school budget at a finance committee meeting, a well-known vocal critic of the school district stood up and said: "Nice presentation Mr. Connolly, but as we all know, figures lie and liars figure."

"Is that an explanation for why you've been scribbling on that scratch pad during my entire presentation, Marvin?" I asked.

It didn't stop him from doing his thing, but it did slow him down a bit, and it signaled to him and to those gathered for the meeting that I wasn't about to be intimidated.

I'm not suggesting that school leaders engage in verbal repartee with hecklers. That's their "shtick," and they love to engage you in it. But at times you have to let them know you know what they are doing and you aren't intimidated. Do it quickly, do it professionally, and move on. Don't get caught up in their game.

TEXTBOOKS

Is there anything more toxic to the cultivation of love of learning than a textbook? Talk about deadly. I've yet to read a textbook that was engaging let alone inspiring. Textbooks are so bland and clinical. They have no writer's voice, and if they have anything that might be called style, it is the style of an office memo.

Handing a student a textbook and expecting him to get engaged with it is like handing someone a glass of sand and expecting him to slake his thirst with it. Give students books written by historians, by scientists and science writers, by artists, by economists, and by writers. Please rescue them from the toxins of textbooks.

DETACHMENT

One afternoon I walked into the office of a principal colleague. He was slumped over his desk, his head cradled in his hands. We talked. He told me how his day had gone. The whole day it seemed had been worn away by one person after another coming into his office with one problem after another. He was exhausted and dejected.

He was a new administrator and I remember describing how a principal's day can go using the following metaphor.

A principal arrives at work early trying to catch up on things before others arrive. He settles in and begins to work and then there is a knock on his door. He looks up and sees someone carrying a ten-pound sack of rocks on his back. The visitor comes in, hands the principal the sack, and walks out relieved that he no longer has to bear its burden. As he exits another person stands in the doorway with his ten-pound sack of rocks.

And so it goes for the principal. By the end of the day the principal has 150 pounds of rocks on his shoulders and fifteen people are walking to their cars relieved of their burdens. The point of the story was, I told him, that a principal cannot emotionally hope to shoulder every problem someone brings to him. A principal has to cultivate a certain emotional detachment in his job or before long he won't even have the energy to crawl to his car at the end of a day.

Detachment doesn't mean we don't care; it simply means we are not going to get emotionally wrapped up in every problem that someone brings to us even as we work to solve it. It means also that we recognize that we don't own some of the problems people bring to us and that while we listen empathetically to them we refuse to make the mistake of shouldering their burden. It also means we recognize we can't solve every problem someone brings to us—even if we'd like to. Detachment isn't easy to cultivate but it is essential if a principal hopes to survive.

A CRITICAL APPROACH OFTEN
BRINGS AN UNDESIRED RESULT

Frustrated by his son's tendency to color his comments with purple expressions, a father called him into the kitchen one day.

"Son, I'm concerned that the language you use will one day get you into trouble." The son acknowledged the problem, but confessed that, while he had tried, he couldn't control the problem.

"I have an idea," the father said handing the boy a bag of spikes and a hammer. "Every time I hear you use one of your offensive expressions I'm going to send you to the backyard to pound one of these spikes into the trunk of that big oak tree there. That will serve as a reminder of your mistake." The boy agreed to give it a try.

A month later the father looked out at the oak tree and saw it covered with spikes and the bag that contained the spikes empty. Dismayed he called his son into the kitchen.

"Son, I apologize; I've suggested the wrong approach to this problem. From now on when I notice that you've gone a while without using one of those expressions, I'm going to send you out to the backyard to pull one of those spikes out of that oak."

Several weeks later the father was enjoying his morning coffee in the kitchen when he happened to look out at the oak tree, where only three spikes remained.

I'm reminded of this story when I see reformers adopt a punitive approach to trying to bring about change in schools—or any organization for that matter.

MAKE YOUR POINT WITH STORYTELLING

There's nothing quite as effective as a good story to drive home a point. People remember stories long after they've forgotten the logical arguments you've tried to make.

23

We Are the Lucky Ones

I remember when I got my first teaching job back in 1965. One of the first things I did was to share my excitement with my Aunt Sarah. Aunt Sarah was my mentor. I knew she'd be pleased that I'd been hired by the local high school, a choice assignment. As I expected, she was thrilled. After reading the letter announcing my appointment, she beamed, gave me a big hug, and said: "I'm so proud of you Michael, and one day you'll be a principal."

Uh, oh.

Oh no, I thought, who would ever want a job like that?

And yet, fifteen years later I found myself accepting a position as an assistant principal and three years after that I had my first job as a principal. To be sure, during my eighteen years as a principal in three schools in the United States and four international schools, I've found myself at times wondering: *Why would anyone want this job?*

But after eighteen years as a school leader, I now recognize that, despite the fact that our jobs can be frustrating and challenging, we are the lucky ones. We are the lucky ones because, when all is said and done, we have jobs that are worth doing; and they would be worth doing even if we weren't paid for doing them.

Imagine the frustration of working in a field where the only reason you would even consider doing the work you did was for the money; making cigarettes or working in the field of advertising jump to mind. Or imagine being a skilled engineer and knowing you could build a product that was rugged, dependable, and durable but because you work for a company that plans obsolescence into its products, you're condemned to creating things that break down before they should. How awful it must be to have a job like that.

And then there is us and our jobs as educational leaders. A student in the international school where I last served as a principal recently highlighted the importance of educators' leadership in the lives of others in an address he made to international teachers and administrators. He was speaking at the conference as one of three winners of a Global Citizenship award. In his address, Yeon Duk told about 1,500 educators gathered at the conference the following story.*

One day a son came to see his father. He was tired and frustrated. He complained to his father about how difficult life had become and confessed that he just wanted to give up. His father, who was a chef, pulled a chair up for his son and invited him to sit down. When his son was seated, the father took three pots of water and placed each one on a stove to boil. When the water had come to a boil, he took a carrot and cut it up into the first pot. Into the second pot he put an egg and into the third pot he put some ground-up coffee. After a few minutes he said to his son, "Come on over here, son; I want to show you something."

As they stood looking at the pots boiling on the stove, the father said to his son: "What do you see?" Impatiently the son replied: "I see three pots: one with carrots, one with an egg, and one with coffee."

"Look closer," his father said; "Can you see:

When the carrots were subjected to the boiling water, they became soft.

When the egg was subjected to the boiling water, it became hard.

But the coffee . . . ah son, when the coffee was poured into the boiling water, it changed the water."

Yeon Duk concluded his address to the gathered educational leaders with these words: "Ladies and gentlemen, you are the ones who show us, your students, that we have the power to change the water."

Yes, despite the fact that those of us who serve as leaders in education have jobs that can be depleting and, at times, discouraging, we are the lucky ones. We have the power to teach people that they can transform their lives and the world. Let us never forget that.

---

* Yeon Duk found the chef story on a poster I kept in my office. The poster is titled *Attitude* and the story is by Charles Swindoll.

Appendix 1

SSIS Mission Statement and Core Values

Saigon South International School (SSIS) is a college preparatory school committed to the intellectual and personal development of each student in preparation for a purposeful life as a global citizen.

CORE VALUES

SSIS believes in and promotes:

- *Academic Excellence*—A challenging academic program based on American standards, that teaches the student how to think, to learn to problem solve, and to work individually and in teams while acquiring a foundational knowledge base of the world.
- *Sense of Self*—A community atmosphere in which each student can gain a sense of who he or she is in the world; to develop self-confidence, strong character, conviction, leadership abilities, grace, courage, the desire to be a lifelong learner, and the commitment to achieve excellence in all he does.
- *Dedicated Service*—A view that looks beyond oneself to the assets and needs of the surrounding community and the world and finds fulfillment in unlocking potential in the service of humankind. The model SSIS graduate will demonstrate a caring attitude, be environmentally aware, and persevere for the good of the community.
- *Balance in Life*—An academic program that promotes an appreciation for all of life and seeks to balance the sciences with the humanities;

academics with the arts; mental wholeness with physical, social, and spiritual wholeness; and future career with family relationships.

- *Respect for All*—A perspective that each individual is a person of worth.

Appendix 2

Some Simple Guidelines for Parents about Homework

- Agree upon a time and a place where homework/study will be done each day/evening Monday through Thursday and Sunday. (These are days that are followed by a school day.) Friday and Saturday can be days of rest.
- This agreement should be with the understanding that homework/study will be done each of these nights. You are establishing the habit of study not just a time for it.
- Study time should be no fewer than 30 minutes and on most nights no more than 90 minutes. (The difficulty of some assignments may on some few nights require more than 90 minutes.)
- Do not hover over your youngster during this time, but be monitoring and be aware of what your son or daughter is doing during this time.
- Under no circumstances should you be doing the homework for your youngster. And you should not be spending a great deal of time assisting your son or daughter in the completion of homework. If your youngster has to ask more than a few clarifying questions on an assignment, he or she needs to go back to the teacher for assistance the next day. Learning to ask for assistance from a teacher about something a student doesn't understand is also an important life skill.
- If you have encouraged your youngster to ask a teacher for help, ask the following day if he or she has done this and have him or her explain what he or she learned. Some students forget to ask or are simply reluctant to acknowledge they need help.
- If you can manage this (and you should make an effort to do so), sit down and read a book of your own during your youngster's study

time, do the bills, work on a report for the office, or some other adult homework task. This is modeling and it is a powerful teaching tool.

WHEN YOUR CHILD SAYS "I DON'T HAVE ANY HOMEWORK" OR "I FINISHED ALL MY HOMEWORK AT SCHOOL"

- Ask to see your child's homework organizer (notebook). Check to see if there are any assignments due. Ask to see all completed homework. Check to see if he or she has any long-term assignments (due later than the next day) that your child could be working on.
- Many teachers put their weekly homework assignments on a Web site. The information about their respective Web sites can be found in newsletters each team puts out or is communicated to you by your child's teachers. If your child's homework assignments are on a Web site, check it often.
- If your child has indeed finished all homework assignments or has none due the following day, here are things you should suggest he or she do during agreed upon study time:

  - Read ahead in his or her textbooks.
  - Do some journal writing. (Most classes have journals or learning logs and teachers always encourage students to be writing in them.)
  - Skill-building exercises using the Web or computer programs (e.g., math tutor, typing tutor, etc.). If you know that your child needs additional skill-building exercise beyond what they have in classes, teachers can provide you with some good Web sites or recommend some computer programs where they can practice needed skills.
  - Do some additional reading for pleasure and learning. Teachers have recommended reading lists for young people from the librarian and language arts department.

A PARENT'S HOMEWORK OBSERVATION CHECKLIST

- Does my child write daily class assignments in a homework organizer in a manner he or she (and I) can understand? Does he or she include the date the assignment is due?
- Does my child bring home all the books and materials he or she needs to complete homework assignments?
- Is my child's three-ring binder neat and well organized or are many papers loose and falling out of it?

- Does my child regularly remember to bring completed homework assignments to class the day they are due, or do I often find them left behind after he or she has departed for school?
- When I examine my child's completed homework assignments do they appear thoughtfully and carefully done? Are they neat, legible, and well presented?
- Does my child know how to attack long-term assignments or projects? Does my child know how to break these assignments down into smaller tasks and work on the individual tasks one at a time or does he or she wait until the night before the assignment is due and then rush to try to complete the assignment all at once?

References

Auden, W.H. & Pearson, N.H. (1968). *Victorian Poets: Tennyson to Yeats*. New York: The Viking Press.

Barth, R. (1991). *Improving Schools from Within: Teachers, Parents and Principals Can Make the Difference*. San Francisco: Jossey-Bass.

———. (2001). *Learning by Heart*. San Francisco: Jossey-Bass.

Batstone, D. (2003). *Saving the Corporate Soul & (Who Knows) Maybe Your Own*. San Francisco: Jossey-Bass.

Bombeck, E. http://www.the parentsite.corn/parenting/quotes.asp.

Brady, J. (1988). *"Popping the Questions": Writers Digest Handbook of Magazine Article Writing*. Cincinnati, OH: Writers Digest Books.

Bridges, W. (1991). *Managing Transitions*. Reading, MA: Addison-Wesley.

Bridges, W. (2003). *Managing from Within: Making the Most of Change*. Cambridge, MA: DaCapo Press.

Brooks, J. S. (2005). *The Dark Side of School Reform: Teaching in the Space between Reality and Utopia*. Lanham, MD: Rowman & Littlefield.

Brown, J. L. & Cerylle, A. (1999). *The Hero's Journey: How Educators Can Transform School and Improve Learning*. Alexandria, VA: ASCD.

Cameron, J. (1992). *The Artist's Way: A Spiritual Path to Higher Creativity*. New York: Penguin Putnam Press.

Council on Competitiveness (2007). *Five for the Future*. Washington, D.C.: author.

Council on Competitiveness (2007). *Winning the Skills Race*. Washington, D.C.: author.

Covey, S. R. (1989). *The Seven Habits of Highly Effective People*. New York: Free Press.

Diver, C. (November 2005). "Is There Life After Rankings?" *The Atlantic* online, available at: www.theatlantic.com/doc/print200511/shunning-college-rankings.

Durden, W. G. (2004). *Leadership, Language Study, and Global Sensibility*. EARCOS 2004 Keynote Address, available at: www.dickinson.edu/about/president/earcosprt.html.

Estes, R. (1996). *The Tyranny of the Bottom Line: Why Corporations Make Good People Do Bad Things*. San Francisco: Berrett-Koehler.

Evans, R. (1996). *The Human Side of School Change*. San Francisco: Jossey-Bass.

Flaherty, R. http://thinkexist.com/quotation/there-s_a_saying_among_prospectors--go_out/224334.html

Friedman, T. L. (2006). *The World Is Flat*. New York: Farrar, Straus and Giroux.

Frost, R. (1992). *You Come Too: Favorite Poems for Young Readers*. New York: Scholastic Inc.

Hargraves, A. & Fullan, M. G. (1998). *What's Worth Fighting for Out There?* New York: Teachers College Press.

Hole, S. & McEntree, G. H. (May 1999). "Reflection Is at the Heart of Practice." *Educational Leadership*: (Volume 56, Number 8, pp. 34–37)

Institute for Alternative Futures. (2006). *Vision 2021: A Journey Into the Leadership Future*, available at NAESP Web site, www.naesp.org.

Kelehear, Z. (2006). *The Art of Leadership: Choreography of Human Understanding*. Lanham, MD: Rowman & Littlefield.

King, S. (2000). *On Writing, a Memoir of the Craft*. New York: Seribner.

Lewis, C. S. (1960). *The World's Last Night and Other Essays*. New York: Harcourt Brace Jovanovich.

Merton, T. (1955). *No Man Is an Island*. Orlando, FL: Harcourt.

Moffett, J. (1994). *The Universal Schoolhouse: Spiritual Awakening Through Education*. San Francisco: Jossey-Bass.

National Commission on Excellence in Education (1983). *A Nation at Risk: The Imperative for Educational Reform*. Washington, D.C.: U.S. Government Printing Office.

O'Hara-Devereau, M. (2004). *Navigating the Badlands: Thriving in a Decade of Radical Transformation*. San Francisco: Jossey-Bass.

Palmer, P. J. (1998). *The Courage to Teach: Exploring the Inner Landscape of a Teacher's Life*. San Francisco: Jossey-Bass.

Postman, N. (1996). *The End of Education: Redefining the Value of School*. New York: Vintage Books.

Raybum, S. http://www.brainyquote.com/quotes/authors/s/sam_rayburn.html

Schon, D. A. (1983). *The Reflective Practitioner*. New York: Basic Books Inc.

Schumacher, E. F. (1973). *Small Is Beautiful: Economics as if People Mattered*. New York: Harper & Row.

Smith, D. K. (1996). *Taking Charge of Change*. Reading, MA: Addison-Wesley.

Toffler, A. (1971). *Future Shock*. New York: Bantam Books.

Tuchman, B. (1981). *Practicing History*. New York: Ballantine Books.

Vail, P. (1989). *Managing as a Performing Art: New Ideas for a World of Chaotic Change*. San Francisco: Jossey-Bass.

Webster, M. (1968). *New World Dictionary of the American Language*. Cleveland, OH: World Publishing Co.

White, J. "How to Live Happily Through the Teenage Years: You Don't Need a Barrel." http://www.crosswalk.com/parenting/teens/506220/

Zhao, Y. (March/April 2007). "Education in a Flat World: Implications of Global Education." *Edge* (Volume 2, Number 4).

About the Author

Mike Connolly has worked as a high school, middle school, and upper elementary school principal in urban, suburban, and rural school districts in the United States and in prestigious international schools in Thailand, Costa Rica, the Netherlands, and Vietnam. Connolly is a graduate of the University of Massachusetts at Lowell with a BA in English. He has a master's degree in American Literature from Salem State College and a master's degree in School Administration from Antioch New England College.

Connolly's articles on education have appeared in national and international journals including *Principal* magazine, *The International Educator*, *The New England League of Middle Schools Journal*, *IS* magazine, *The Journal of Innovative Teaching, Principal Matters* (Australian), and the *NAESP Principals' Electronic Newsdesk*. Connolly has designed and presented staff development workshops in Europe and Asia as well as in the United States. He has taught seminars and courses at universities in the Netherlands and Thailand. He can be contacted at secondcareer2007@yahoo.com.

ML   11-15